# The 5 P's For a Perfect Meeting

# (A Step-by-step Guide to Navigate Meetings Like a Pro)

Also by Elizabeth J Tucker:

Simply Stress (Stress Management Exercises, Strategies and Techniques)

The 7 Deadly Sins of Chairing Meetings (Let's Get it Right Every Time)

Success Starts Here (Things Every Minute Taker Should Know)

Publisher: Shepherd Creative Learning

# The 5 P's For a Perfect Meeting

## (A Step-by-step Guide to Navigate Meetings Like a Pro)

### By: Elizabeth J Tucker

# Copyright:

## Publisher's Note:

The author has made every reasonable attempt to achieve complete accuracy of the content in this book prior to going to press. The publisher, the editor and the author cannot accept responsibility for any errors or omissions, however caused.

You should use this information as you see fit, and at your own risk. You should adjust your use of this information and recommendations accordingly.

Finally, use your own wisdom as guidance. Nothing in this Guide is intended to replace common sense, legal, or other professional advice. This book is meant to inform and entertain the reader.

No responsibility for loss or damage occasioned to any person acting, or refraining from action, as a result of the material in this publication can be accepted by the publisher, the author or the editor.

## Dedication:

The book is dedicated to Dennis Shepherd (my lovely partner), and Rosemary Tucker and Geoffrey Tucker (my hugely supportive parents).

This book is also dedicated to all the people who have attended our Chairing Successful Meetings and Minute Taking Made Easy training workshops. It's also dedicated to all the chairmen and women that I've talked to in the course of my research. Thank you for sharing your views, experiences and questions to help make this book possible.

# About the Author:

Elizabeth is based near the Cotswolds. She has several roles. Elizabeth is a successful author, business consultant, holistic life coach and stress management consultant.

Elizabeth is an innovative presenter with an engaging manner. She has spent many years helping individuals and organisations achieve their goals. Elizabeth writes her books based on her considerable business knowledge and experience.

She describes herself as an enthusiastic go-getter with a passion for helping others reach their full potential or achieve their goals. Elizabeth uses her own unique blend of insight, wisdom and humour in her work. Her catchphrase is "inspiration and support when you need it".

As well as a successful corporate career she has owned and managed several businesses. Since starting her own business in 2003 she has had the privilege of working with a diverse client base. Her clients have included The Chartered Institute of Housing, Blue Chip companies, the British Army, charities, social housing providers, SME and start-up businesses, and personal clients.

Elizabeth is currently working on a project to create a series of self-help business books. These will be available as paperbacks and Kindle books. You can find out when these are published by viewing her LinkedIn profile (liz-tucker/10/531/68/) or following her on Twitter (@liztucker03).

# Table of Contents

# Preface

How much do you really know about meetings? We all spend hundreds of hours in meetings each year, but we often don't think about the five P's for a perfect meeting. In case you're wondering, the five P's are - preparation, purpose, process, performance and pay-off.

Meetings have a vital role to play in the success of all organisations. Unfortunately, vast sums of money are wasted on ineffective meetings each year. This is usually because the organiser or chairperson doesn't know that protocols and good practices exist for meetings.

I've been involved with meetings for most of my adult life. My experience has included being an attendee, chairperson and minute taker. I've been involved in formal, business and informal meetings, so I know a thing or two about meetings.

I was conducting research into what readers want from a book on minute taking when I was prompted to write this book. I was asked a huge variety of questions about the topic of meetings. It quickly became clear that there was too much information for one book.

Therefore, this book is part of a series of three books covering the broad topic of meetings and minute taking.

This book is entitled The 5 P's to a Perfect Meeting (A Step-by-step Guide to Navigate Meetings Like a Pro). This book will guide you through the end-to-end meeting process. Poor planning and preparation lead to poor meetings and sometimes no benefits. The titles of the other two books in the series are:

1. The 7 Deadly Sins of Chairing Meetings (Let's Get it Right Every Time). If you've never had any formal chairing meetings training you've probably picked up some good practices and some bad habits

2. Success Starts Here (Things Every Minute Taker Should Know). This practical guide deals with the role of the meeting secretary and the minute taker. It will help the reader to create clear, concise and accurate minutes time after time

Each book is designed to be a practical guide. You will find handy hints and exercises throughout each book. The exercises will test your knowledge or provide you with an opportunity to think about how you and your organisation currently operate.

I hope these three books will provide you with some practical guidance on the broad topic of meetings. Meetings are probably a key part of your working week so it makes sense to develop an extensive knowledge on the subject.

# 1. Introduction

We all have our own opinions about what makes a good meeting. Interestingly, no two people will share exactly the same views. The one thing everyone agrees on is the chairperson is largely responsible for the success or not of the meeting.

Of course there are many elements to successful meetings, but a key element is effective communication. Professor Albert Mehrabian pioneered the Mehrabian Communication Model that is still used today.

Part of his research looked at the most effective means of communication (written, verbal and non-verbal). His research suggests the written word only carries 7% of the true meaning and feeling of the message. This immediately presents a case for face-to-face meetings or teleconferences.

His research then goes further to suggest that face-to-face meetings are more effective than teleconferences. According to his research only 38% of the meaning and feeling is carried verbally. He states that 55% of the meaning is carried by facial expressions and non-verbal communication.

Professor Mehrabian doesn't stop there. He goes on to suggest that typical video-conferencing is not as reliable as face-to-face communications either. In fairness to him technology has progressed in leaps and bounds since his original research. The bottom line is meetings play an important role in modern businesses.

So what can you expect from this book? By the end of this book you will be able to:

1. Plan and run effective meetings

2. Be able to calculate the cost of each meeting

3. Use your knowledge to select the right type of agenda for your meetings

4. Understand all the roles and responsibilities associated with meetings

5. Be able to create an agenda template and minutes template for your meetings

6. Create clear, concise and accurate minutes for your meetings

7. Do everything in a timely manner to ensure maximum effectiveness

Meetings are vital for effective leadership, business management, organisational productivity and good communication. However, when was the last time you heard someone say "that was a really good meeting"?

# Exercise: Meetings - Quick Quiz

You might like to test your knowledge before reading this book. This quick quiz will test how much you already know about meetings and minute taking.

**Instructions:**

Read each statement and circle your answers.

1. The chairperson is always the most senior person at the meeting - True/False?

2. Being the chairperson requires specific skills - True/False?

3. To be a good minute taker you need good shorthand or speedwriting skills - True/False?

4. The agenda is just used to provide an idea of the topics to be discussed. It's not written in any specific order - True/False?

5. The task of minute taking should always be assigned to the least senior member of staff as it's an admin role - True/False?

6. The minutes from the previous meeting should be issued with the agenda for the next meeting - True/False?

7. Apologies always appear as '1. Apologies' on the agenda - True/False?

8. Everyone who doesn't attend the meeting should be recorded under 'Apologies' - True/False?

9. Minutes are just a record for those people who attended the meeting - True/False?

10. How many styles of agenda and styles of minutes are there? - three/five/ten

You will find the answers to this quick quiz in the Appendices section at the end of the book.

Meetings are expensive and so need to be a cost-effective use of company time and money. Everyone who attends the meeting should have a specific role to play. No one should ever attend a meeting 'just in case their input is needed'.

In case you're interested I have included instructions to help you calculate the cost of your meetings. I've also included details of each of the four roles involved with meetings.

So, to the 5 P's for a perfect meeting... These are Purpose, preparation, process, performance and pay-off. Obviously purpose is the responsibility of the chairperson. Preparation, process and performance involve everyone who attends the meeting. Pay-off is the reward to you and your organisation for getting it right.

Never again does anyone need to feel a meeting was a waste of time. All you need to do is follow the simple rules set out in The 5 P's For a Perfect Meeting.

## Exercise: My Regular Meetings

Before you go any further you might like to reflect on the meetings you attend. Consider the meetings you attend as a chairperson, minute taker or attendee. There are no right or wrong answers to this exercise. These are just your personal observations.

**Instructions:**

Read each question and then write your answers down

1. How many meetings do you attend, on average, each month?

2. At every meeting do you contribute in some way?

3. Do you ever leave meetings feeling that was a waste of time?

4. What can you do to make these meetings more effective for you?

5. How could your organisation improve meetings e.g. better planning, consistent agenda and minutes style etc?

Before moving on reflect on what you've learnt from this exercise.

# 2. Frequently Asked Questions

In the course of my research I talked to lots of people about their experiences of meetings. Their feedback has been invaluable in creating this chapter. Here are the questions I was asked most often. I've also suggested how to resolve the issues.

**Question/Issue:** I'm not sure how to prepare the agenda. I don't know what order to list things
**Answer:** The good news is all agendas should follow the same order. This is - Apologies, Welcome, Minutes of the previous meeting, Matters arising, Reports, Main agenda items, Any other business, and Date of next meeting

**Question/Issue:** I'm new to the organisation, and I don't have much knowledge of the meeting I'm taking minutes for
**Answer:** If possible try to attend your first meeting as an observer. If this isn't possible ask the chairperson to brief you. This briefing should include the group dynamics, purpose of the meeting, technical references and jargon, and any expectations the chairperson has of you

**Question/Issue:** If I'm invited to a meeting do I need to attend?
**Answer:** No. You should only attend meetings if you have something to contribute. If you don't know why you have been invited, ask the chairperson

**Question/Issue:** How long should meetings last?
**Answer:** The length of time will vary from meeting to meeting. The general rule is - meetings should be long enough to cover the business but not longer than necessary. Ideally meetings should be less than two hours as concentration wanes after this

**Question/Issue:** Who is responsible for the agenda?
**Answer:** The chairperson has overall responsibility for what is included on the agenda. Attendees are responsible for putting forward suggestions for discussion. Either the meeting secretary or the chairperson will be responsible for creating the agenda

**Question/Issue:** Do I have to include every agenda item I get a request for?
**Answer:** No. Look at each agenda item and decide whether it should be included or not. For an agenda item to be included it needs to be relevant to the overall purpose of the meeting and the majority of the attendees.

Agenda items that only affect a couple of people should be discussed outside the meeting

**Question/Issue:** I don't know whether a meeting is really necessary or not. How do I decide?
**Answer:** Think about how many people are impacted by the issue to be discussed. Will it be quicker and more efficient to have a short meeting rather than several days or weeks of telephone calls and emails? Meetings can be an efficient and effective use of time. Equally, many are a waste of time and money

**Question/Issue:** Do we need to have an agenda for every meeting?
**Answer:** Yes. If you decide not to create an agenda then you should have a list of topics for discussion. Otherwise your meeting is open to abuse as people will see it as an opportunity to discuss anything and everything. Remember, meetings are expensive and so need to provide value for money

**Question/Issue:** How frequently should we meet?
**Answer:** You need to consider each meeting individually. Some meetings will need to be weekly or monthly. Other meetings may be occasional, or even just a one-off meeting. There are no fixed rules regarding frequency

**Question/Issue:** I've booked a meeting, but now I don't know whether we really need it
**Answer:** If you don't think you need a meeting then you probably don't. Cancel it. You can always reschedule the meeting at a later date if you decide it's necessary

**Question/Issue:** Should the chair of the meeting be the most senior member of staff?
**Answer:** No. It needs to be the most relevant person (usually the person who decided the meeting was necessary)

**Question/Issue:** How do I know which style of agenda is required
**Answer:** Your organisation may have a policy. If not, think about how formal the meeting is. Board meetings often use a full agenda, but for most business meetings the basic agenda works well

**Question/Issue:** We generally issue the agenda at the start of the meeting, but I've been told this is the wrong thing to do. When should the agenda be issued?
**Answer:** Issuing the agenda at the start of the meeting doesn't give anyone time to prepare. The agenda should be issued at least four

working days in advance for monthly meetings. For weekly meetings the agenda should be issued at least three working days before the meeting

**Question/Issue:** At our team meetings some people don't say anything. What should we do about this?
**Answer:** The rule is very simple - contribute or don't attend. The chairperson should try to draw them into the discussions. If they steadfastly refuse to participate they should stop attending

**Question/Issue:** The same people do all the talking at our meetings. As a group should we say something?
**Answer:** No. It's the chairperson's responsibility to tackle this issue. Have a discreet word with the chairperson outside the meeting

**Question/Issue:** Can we rotate the role of chairperson and minute taker?
**Answer:** Yes. This provides a good skills development opportunity. Make sure the acting chairperson and minute taker know well in advance. Never spring it on them at the start of the meeting

**Question/Issue:** Actions keep being carried forward from one meeting to the next. We never seem to close down old actions
**Answer:** This is not good practice. Carry actions forward once if really necessary. If the action still isn't complete it can't be that important. Close the action down with a covering note stating the action is being closed because it hasn't been completed and is no longer relevant

**Question/Issue:** Does the numbering on the agenda and minutes really need to match?
**Answer:** Yes. This is part of the audit trail

**Question/Issue:** Do we need to stick to the order of the agenda during the meeting, or can we switch things around?
**Answer:** You should stick to the order of the agenda. Think carefully about the required order when creating the agenda. Switching the order makes unnecessary extra work for the minute taker

**Question/Issue:** Is it alright to record the meeting instead of taking minutes?
**Answer:** Yes as long as you have everyone's permission to do so. You also need to be confident that the recording equipment won't fail. Just be aware that if it fails you will have no record of the meeting

**Question/Issue:** How should I record who was present and who was absent in the meeting?

**Answer:** Always start with those present. List the chairperson and then the minute taker. The reader will automatically know who chaired the meeting and took the minutes without you needing to write a separate note. Next, list the attendees in alphabetical order by last name. Apologies follow those present. These should also be listed in alphabetical order. Finally, identify anyone who was absent. These are the people who were expected to attend but didn't turn up or send their apologies

**Question/Issue:** Does the chairperson need to have a different agenda to everyone else?

**Answer:** No, but this more detailed agenda does make the task of chairing easier. It also helps ensure and efficient meeting. Personally I would never consider chairing a formal or business meeting without the chairperson's agenda. Informal meetings are different as you may not have an agenda to start with

# 3. The Real Cost of Meetings

Be under no illusion, meetings are expensive. If a meeting is necessary then it should be structured and properly recorded to provide value for money. Meetings need to be the best use of employees' time and company funds.

Unfortunately, a lot of time and money is wasted on meetings every year. This is one business efficiency that all organisations should look at periodically. Just about every organisation could make savings by creating some good practice guidelines for meetings.

How often have you been to a meeting just because someone thought it 'was a good idea to have a meeting'? In this scenario the person suggesting the meeting has usually failed to think about the cost. People who don't think about the cost often put as little thought into the rest of the planning of their meetings.

I thought you might find it helpful to have a meeting calculator. Next time you are considering having a meeting, allow the meeting calculator to help you decide.

The instructions below will enable you to calculate the cost of each meeting you have. This calculation does not take into account the time spent on preparing for the meeting (agenda etc). Also, it doesn't include the time take to produce and issue the minutes. These are added costs that should be considered.

How to calculate the cost of a meeting

Step 1: Add up the annual salaries of everyone attending the meeting £

Step 2: Add 25% to this figure. This represents the organisation's overheads £

Step 3: Divide the answer from step 2 by 52 weeks £

Step 4: Divide the answer from step 3 by the number of hours in your working week (e.g. 37 hours). This will give you the hourly cost of this meeting £

Step 5: Multiply the answer from step 4 by the length of the meeting (e.g. 2 hours) £

Step 6: Add any other costs (e.g. room hire, refreshments etc) £

Step 7: Add the answers from steps 5 and 6. This will give you the cost of this meeting £

Total = £

To help make this clearer I have created a fictitious meeting with five attendees. Our fictitious meeting is schedule for two hours:

Step 1: The combined salary of our five attendees is £156,000

Step 2: £156,000 x 25% = £39,000. This figure is the cost of the overheads for this meeting

Step 3: £156,000 (salaries) + £39,000 (overheads) = £195,000

Step 4: £195,000 ÷ 52 weeks = £3,750

Step 5: £3,750 ÷ 37 hours (the number of hours our staff work each week) = £101.35. This is the hourly cost of our meeting

Step 6: Our meeting is scheduled for 2 hours. £101.35 x 2 hours = £202.72

Step 7: There are no additional costs for our meeting. Therefore, the cost of a two-hour meeting for five members of staff = £202.72

This figure doesn't take into account the time and effort that went into planning the meeting. Also, it doesn't take into account the time to type, review and issue the minutes. These tasks could double the cost of your meeting.

At any one time there is usually more than one meeting going on, which demonstrates the point that meetings are expensive. They need to be a productive use of time and company funds.

Think very carefully about who needs to attend. Don't be tempted to invite people who might be useful, or might be interested in the meeting.

Sometimes we sit through an entire meeting when we only really need to attend for part of the meeting. I hope this has given you food for thought.

I believe meetings play a vital role in modern businesses, but there is no excuse for poor planning and execution. Time is money for any organisation so be cost-aware when planning your meetings.

# 4. Types of Meeting

Meetings fall into three categories. These are formal meetings, business meetings and informal meetings. In your role as chairperson it's important to understand the type of meeting you are chairing. This will affect the way you plan and conduct proceedings during your meeting.

## 4.1 Skills of Effective Chairmen/Women

There are lots of different types of formal meeting. I have provided a summary of the most common formal meetings for your information.

### Annual General Meeting (AGM)
As the name suggests, this is an annual meeting. It's often a mandatory meeting, comprising the company's directors and shareholders. The chairperson will have been elected according to company rules. Chairing an AGM is a weighty role.

### Extraordinary General Meeting (EGM)
An EGM can be called at any time between AGMs if shareholder approval is required. The same rules apply to the meeting as apply to AGMs.

### Board Meetings
A board meeting is attended by the board of a company, usually directors. These are often regular meetings, and the purpose is to discuss company business. If you are the chairperson for board meetings you will have been elected according to company rules. This is a very senior role.

### A Standing Committee
A standing committee is a sub-committee of the company's board. This committee has delegated tasks, and meets regularly to discuss these. The committee can use its discretion to choose the chairperson. Whoever is selected will be a senior member of staff.

### One-off Committee
This committee is set up by the board to look at a single issue. The committee can meet as frequently or infrequently as they choose. The committee can use its discretion to choose the chairperson. Due to the nature of the project the chairperson will be a senior member of staff.

### Public Meetings
As the name suggests, public meetings are open to anyone. Local government and private action groups often use this type of meeting. The

committee leading the public meeting will select the chairperson. Nominate a strong chairperson for this type of meeting as the public don't always know the rules of engagement in meetings.

Generally you won't know in advance how many people will be present at the meeting. This can be a little daunting for inexperienced chairmen/women.

### Conference
Most conferences are private affairs but some are open to the public. The chairperson's primary role is often to act as a facilitator for the meeting.

Conferences generally involve several presentations, which are introduced by the chairperson. Although this style of meeting allows little room for discussion the chairperson may hold a question and answer session. He/she will invite questions from the audience and select one of the presenters to answer.

### External Meetings
External meetings involve people from your own organisation along with representatives from outside the organisation. Due to the dynamics of the group you need to elect a strong and capable chairperson to run the meeting. Meetings that involve internal and external parties often involve hidden agendas.

## 4.2 Business Meetings

Business or workplace meetings are the most common form of meetings that most people chair. Business meetings are vital for effective leadership, business management and good communication throughout the organisation.

Not all business meetings are internal only. You may have business meetings with clients and/or suppliers. Treat these like any other business meeting but be aware that attendees may have their own agendas.

Every business meeting you chair should serve a purpose. The first task is to identify why you need a meeting. I often hear "it seemed like a good idea at the time" or "we've been doing this for years". These are not good reasons to have a business meeting.

If you decide a meeting is necessary then your next task is to identify the aim and objectives of the meeting. Do this before considering who the attendees should be.

The more carefully you plan your meeting the more efficient and effective it will be. Always keep your meetings as small as possible but don't exclude people who can make a useful contribution.

Although business meetings generally involve a group of people you could have a one-to-one business meeting. Due to the nature of performance appraisals, a business meeting is ideal. It will provide the structure needed for this type of meeting.

## 4.3 Informal Meetings

Just like formal meetings, informal meetings come in many guises. Whatever form your informal meeting takes make sure you do it away from your desk. Psychologically this makes it easier to end the meeting and walk away. Research shows that meetings around someone's desk tend to go on longer than necessary.

Even though you are having an informal meeting, think about location. A fruitful discussion is less likely if the attendees feel uncomfortable. Therefore, always opt for as much privacy as possible. This will encourage attendees to participate freely.

Whether your meeting is formal or informal, you still need a chairperson and, ideally, an agenda. A meeting without a chairperson becomes a free-for-all and generally lacks structure or direction. If you are chairing an informal meeting without an agenda use lots of eye contact. This will help you retain control of the meeting.

### Impromptu Meetings
This style of meeting can be very helpful for reaching decisions quickly. This is an ideal meeting for small groups that have an issue that needs a speedy resolution. Ideally you don't want a group size of more than four people for impromptu meetings.

### Ideas Sharing Meetings
Some like to call these 'ideas sharing' meetings. Others prefer to refer to them as 'brainstorming' or 'thought showers'. Whatever you call it, they all amount to the same thing - a very short meeting for generating ideas.

For maximum impact these meetings should be no longer than 30-40 minutes and high energy. Throw an initial idea into the melting pot and then encourage a speedy flow of suggestions.

Ideas sharing meetings are good for creating new ideas or generating quick ideas for solutions to existing problems. Even though this is an informal meeting, still ask someone to take notes. Otherwise the output is likely to be forgotten.

In order to make this type of meeting successful ensure the group consists of people with different expertise. Try to keep the group size small for the best results.

If you are chairing this style of meeting it's important not to criticise or judge the ideas presented. This would put people off contributing. The time for judging and feasibility is after the meeting. For now, just capture every suggestion with an open mind.

Informal meetings are often used for daily or weekly project planning or progress updates. This style of meeting is excellent for keeping everyone informed.

Note: if this meeting is likely to take more than 60 minutes consider scheduling a business meeting.

# 5. The Meeting Lifecycle

Regardless of the frequency (monthly, weekly, annually or ad-hoc), every meeting should go through the same cycle. Only the timescale will be different.

Monthly or less frequent meetings (including one-off meetings) should apply the same timescales. Only weekly meetings will be treated differently. In this case the timescale will be shorter.

The following is good practice in the lifecycle of a meeting. Adhering to the meeting cycle will add to the overall effectiveness of the meeting. Adopting good practice guidelines will:

1. Ensure everyone has sufficient opportunity to prepare for the meeting

2. Ensure all relevant documents are issued in a timely manner

3. Make the minute takers role easier on the day of the meeting

4. Ensure the minutes are issued in a timely manner

5. Increase the chances of outstanding actions being completed before the next meeting

Sometimes the role of meeting secretary and minute taker is done by the same person. If the meeting secretary and minute taker are different people it's important they work as a team. This will ensure greater efficiency before, during and after the meeting.

## 5.1 Monthly or Less Frequent Meetings

**8 working days before the meeting** - is the deadline for submitting agenda items, reports and any other papers. These should be sent to the meeting secretary. If you are the meeting secretary, don't get into the habit of accepting late agenda items.

If absolutely necessary, late submissions can be dealt with under 'Any other business'. Ideally late agenda items should be added to the agenda for the next meeting.

**5-7 working days before the meeting** - the meeting secretary drafts the agenda. The chairperson should approve the agenda before it's issued. This adds to the overall effectiveness and efficiency of the meeting.

The meeting secretary is also expected to verify that all outstanding actions have been completed. If not, he/she should get an update on the outstanding actions. This information should be shared with the chairperson and minute taker before the next meeting.

**4-5 working days before the meeting** - issue the agenda and any other documents to be discussed at the meeting. Everyone who is expected to attend the meeting should receive a copy of all the relevant papers. This will enable them to prepare for the meeting.

The agenda should be cross-referenced to indicate which papers/reports relate to each agenda item. This aids the efficiency of the meeting and provides an accurate audit trail.

**1 working day before the meeting** - the chairperson and the minute taker should have a short briefing session.

The purpose of this briefing is to discuss the content of the meeting, any potential problem areas and style of minutes. It's also an opportunity to identify any help either party is likely to need during the meeting.

**Day of the meeting** - the minute taker should take as many notes as he/she feels is necessary. The notes should include all the important discussion points, the actions, action owner and date for completing any actions.

**I working day after the meeting** - the minute taker types a draft set of minutes.

The minutes should be an accurate record of the meeting. This is not an opportunity for personal views. The minutes should be as near complete as possible at this stage.

**2-3 working days after the meeting** - the minutes should be reviewed by the chairperson. He/she is checking for accuracy and political correctness; nothing else. The chairperson should not add extra information unless it was part of the discussion and has been left out of the minutes.

The chairperson should not amend the minutes to reflect his/her own personal writing style. Also, he/she should not use this as an opportunity to include their personal views.

**Not later than 5 working days after the meeting** - circulate a copy of the minutes to all attendees. Those who sent apologies are entitled to a copy of the minutes.

## 5.2 Weekly Meetings

**4 working days before the meeting** - is the deadline for submitting agenda items, reports and any other papers. These should be sent to the meeting secretary. If you are the meeting secretary, don't get into the habit of accepting late agenda items.

**3 working days before the meeting** - the meeting secretary drafts the agenda. The chairperson should approve the agenda before it's issued.

The meeting secretary is also expected to check that all outstanding actions have been completed. If not, he/she should get an update on the outstanding actions. This information should be shared with the chairperson and minute taker before the next meeting.

Issue the agenda and any other papers/reports to be discussed at the meeting. Everyone who is expected to attend the meeting should receive a copy of all the relevant papers. This will enable everyone to prepare for the meeting.

**1 working day before the meeting** - the chairperson and minute taker should have a short briefing session. This briefing is just to identify any issues or matters either of you needs to be made aware of.

**Day of the meeting** - the minute taker should take as many notes as he/she feels is necessary. The notes should include the important discussion points, the actions, action owner and timescale for completing actions.

**1 working day after the meeting** - create the minutes today. Due to the tight timescale between meetings It's essential to do this. The minutes should be a factual record of the meeting. The minutes should be as near complete as possible at this stage.

**1-2 working days after the meeting** - the chairperson should review the minutes for accuracy and political correctness. This is not an opportunity for the chairperson to make changes to the minutes. Changes should only be made if the minutes are factually incorrect or there is information missing.

Issue the minutes today. All attendees and those who sent apologies are entitled to a copy of the minutes.

**Handy hint:** No one likes their agenda items to be left off the agenda. If you follow a strict policy of not accepting late agenda items you will find people don't send them to you late.

# Exercise: The Meeting Lifecycle

If you follow the good practice guidelines in this chapter I guarantee the end result will be more efficient meetings. This is good news for you and your organisation.

**Instructions:**

Spend a few minutes having a reality check. Answer the following questions.

1. Does everyone know the cut-off date for sending their agenda items? If not, you might like to consider making everyone aware. This will save the meeting secretary work in the long-run

2. Does the chairperson or meeting secretary regularly accept late agenda items? If so, stop doing this. You won't have time for extra agenda items during the meeting

3. When are your agenda and other documents issued? Are they always issued together?

4. When are the minutes issued?

5. What are you going to do differently in future?

# 6. Roles and Responsibilities

There are potentially four roles in every meeting. Everyone at the meeting will fit into one of the following roles - chairperson, minute taker, attendee or observer. Visitors are classed as attendees.

Not all meetings will have observers or visitors, but all meetings should have a chairperson and minute taker. These roles should be agreed in advance, not at the start of the meeting.

It's good practice to invite new minute takers to observe a meeting before they start. This helps the new minute taker to understand what the meeting is about. It's also an opportunity to get to know the attendees and understand what is expected of the minute taker.

It's difficult to be both chairperson and minute taker or contributor and minute taker. This is also an inefficient use of time as it slows the meeting down. The minute taker should not be expected to contribute to the meeting. Their role is purely minute taking.

If the minute taker is required to contribute, ask someone else to take the minutes for that particular item.

Each role has its own responsibilities before, during and after the meeting. Whatever your role, it's important to know what is expected of you. Apart from observers everyone who attends the meeting should make a positive contribution to the meeting.

**Handy hint:** Ensure the minute taker is appointed before the meeting date. Minute taking can be stressful if you aren't properly prepared.

## 6.1 The Chairperson

Every meeting should have a chairperson. If no-one is appointed to this role the meeting will turn into a free-for-all.

The buck stops here. Ultimately, the chairperson will be responsible for the success or failure of the meeting. If you do chair meetings it's worth taking the time to understand your role and the responsibilities.

Before the meeting:

1. Decide if the meeting is really necessary. Over 50% of meetings are not totally necessary

2. Define the aim and objectives of the meeting

3. Identify the attendees. This should just be people who have something useful to contribute to the meeting. Don't fall into the trap of inviting people 'just in case'

4. Invite the attendees, or arrange for the meeting secretary to do this on your behalf

5. Ensure all attendees know why they have been invited and what is expected of them

6. Advise visitors if they are required for the whole meeting or just part of it. If visitors are only required for part of the meeting confirm what time they need to arrive

7. Tell the meeting secretary which style of agenda you want to use. Note: the Basic Agenda is suitable for most business meetings

8. Approve the agenda before it's issued. This ensures you know what is going to be discussed at the meeting

9. Arrange a short briefing session with the minute taker. This discussion should include any potential problem areas and your preferred style of minutes. Also discuss potential issues or problem attendees, and any help either of you needs during the meeting. Do you want the minute taker to be responsible for timekeeping?

10. Everyone should take responsibility for ensuring they are properly prepared for the meeting. Are you leading any of the discussions? If so, know what you want to say

11. Are you familiar with everything listed on the agenda? If not, do your homework

12. Aim to arrive 15 minutes before the meeting start-time to welcome any visitors or first-time attendees. Brief the minute taker on any last-minute changes

**Handy hint:** Small meetings make it easier to involve everyone in the discussions. Larger groups can be useful for problem solving, but it's difficult to involve everyone if the group is too big.

During the meeting:

1. Introduce anyone who has not attended previously, including visitors

2. Remind everyone of the purpose of the meeting and expected outcomes. This helps to focus everyone's attention

3. Ensure the agenda is adhered to. Ensure the discussions are relevant to the agenda item under discussion

4. Control the discussion time. Failure to do so may mean you don't complete the agenda

5. Ensure that only one person speaks at a time. Think of the minute taker trying to capture the discussion

6. Ensure everyone makes a contribution to the meeting. You may have to draw out quiet attendees and silence talkative ones

7. Manage any difficult attendees and do not allow anyone to hijack the meeting

8. Value everyone's contribution. This encourages people to participate

9. Encourage a free exchange of ideas. This is particularly helpful for creative problem solving

10. Don't allow anyone to ramble on. Think - time is money

11. Resolve arguments, or at least find some merit in everyone's point of view

12. Support the minute taker. This may involve ensuring the minute taker is keeping up with the discussion or summarising what needs to be minuted

13. Keep everyone focused on the current agenda item

After the meeting:

1. Provide support to the minute taker when he/she is creating the minutes by answering any questions

2. Approve the minutes. You should approve the minutes 2-3 days after the meeting

3. Provide support to attendees (if required), to help them complete their actions

4. Confirm who is entitled to a copy of the minutes

## Exercise: My Chairing Skills

Think about the meetings you chair. Take a few moments to reflect on your skills as a chairperson. No matter how good you are, there is always room for a little fine-tuning.

**Instructions:**

Now you've read this section you know what is expected of you before, during and after the meeting. Make three lists:

List 1 - the things I already do (this is an opportunity to give yourself a pat on the back)

List 2 - the things I don't currently do, but should

List 3 - things I will do differently in future. This is your action plan

## 6.2 The Meeting Secretary and the Minute Taker

For the purpose of this book I have assumed the meeting secretary and minute taker are the same person. The meeting secretary is responsible up to the point of issuing the agenda and obtaining the action updates. From here on the minute taker is responsible.

Before the meeting:

1. Book the meeting room and refreshments etc

2. Invite attendees (unless they already know they are expected to attend)

3. Find out which style of agenda should be used for the meeting. Note: the Basic Agenda is suitable for most business meetings

4. Prepare and issue the agenda (see good practice guidelines in chapter 5)

5. Issue all relevant papers to attendees

6. Print copies of the agenda, minutes of the previous meeting and any other documents you might need

7. Prepare your notepad

8. Arrive 15 minutes before the meeting start-time to make sure the room is set up correctly. Discuss any last-minute changes with the chairperson

9. Ask the chairperson who is going to be responsible for time keeping

During the meeting:

1. Make a record of the attendees (including visitors), apologies and anyone who is absent. It's important to separate the absent from apologies as this needs to be a factual record of the meeting

2. Take sufficient notes to enable you to compile clear, concise and accurate minutes. This will be different for everyone

3. As a minimum, make a note of any actions, action owner and completion date. It's helpful to have a short summary of the discussion too

4. If you don't understand the discussion, speak up. Query anything you don't understand before the meeting moves on

5. If you are not an experienced minute taker ask the chairperson to summarise what should be minuted

After the meeting:

1. Clarify any misunderstandings with the chairperson or attendees

2. Type a draft set of minutes as soon as possible after the meeting (not later than 2 working days after the meeting)

3. Pass the draft minutes to the chairperson for approval. He/she should approve the minutes 2-3 working days after the meeting

4. Issue the minutes

5. Follow-up outstanding actions before the next meeting

6. Do not make any amendments to the minutes after they have been issued. Amendments should only be dealt with at the next meeting

**Handy hint:** Once the minutes have been issued they should never be amended until the next meeting, when they will be discussed under 'Minutes of the previous meeting'.

# Exercise: My Experience as a Meeting Secretary or Minute Taker

Think about the meetings you plan or take the minutes for. No matter how good you are, there is always room for a little fine-tuning.

**Instructions:**

Now you've read this section you know what is expected of you before, during and after the meeting. Make three lists:

List 1 - the things I already do (this is an opportunity to give yourself a pat on the back)

List 2 - the things I don't currently do, but should

List 3 - things I will do differently in future. This is your action plan

## 6.3 Attendees and Visitors

Before the meeting:

1. Respond the meeting invitation

2. Visitors, find out if you need to attend the whole meeting or just part of the meeting

3. If you are unable to attend the meeting send your apologies as soon as possible

4. Know why you have been invited to attend the meeting, and what is expected of you. If in doubt, ask

5. Send your agenda items to the meeting secretary before the cut-off date. See chapter 5 for the good practice guidelines

6. Read the agenda and accompanying papers. Make a note of any questions you have so you can raise them during the meeting

7. Complete any actions from the previous meeting. Update the meeting secretary

8. If you are delivering a presentation at the meeting ensure the minute taker has a copy of your presentation. Ideally you should send this to the minute taker in in advance

Handy hint: Not all attendees need to attend the entire meeting. It's fine to invite people for specific agenda items

During the meeting:

1. Arrive on time and properly prepared. It's your responsibility to ensure you have a copy of the agenda and any other documents. Don't expect the minute taker to provide you with copies

2. Make a valid and useful contribution to the meeting. Ensure your comments are relevant to the topic under discussion

3. Treat other attendees with courtesy and respect

4. Advise the chair of any factual errors in the minutes of the previous meeting. This will be dealt with under 'Minutes of the previous meeting' on the agenda

5. Make a note of your actions and the completion date. It's your responsibility to make as many notes as necessary to complete your actions

**Handy hint:** The minute taker will only take limited notes regarding each action. It's each action owners' responsibility to ensure they have all the notes they need/want to complete their actions.

After the meeting:

1. Support the minute taker by clarifying any misunderstandings/answering any questions

2. Read the minutes and make notes of anything that is factually incorrect. Note: spelling mistakes and grammar errors will not be amended. Save your comments for the next meeting

3. Complete your actions on time. Update the minute taker/meeting secretary when your actions have been completed

4. Inform the minute taker if any actions cannot be completed on time. Always give a valid reason for any actions not completed

**Handy hint:** Notifying the meeting secretary when your actions have been completed improves the efficiency of the next meeting.

# Exercise: My Experience as an Attendee/Visitor

If we're honest, we have all been to meetings and not contributed in any way. This is fine if you are there to observe, but this isn't generally the case.

**Instructions:**

Spend a few minutes thinking about the meetings you attend. Answer the following questions honestly:

1. Are you genuinely required at every meeting?

2. Do you always know why you have been invited and what is expected of you?

3. Do you make a contribution at each meeting you attend?

4. If not, why not?

5. Are there any regular meetings you attend that you think are a waste of time? If so, what can you do about it?

6. What are you going to do differently in future?

## 6.4 Observers

Observers are at the meeting to observe, but not participate in, the meeting. Observers are not normally named in the minutes as they haven't contributed in any way.

If you have observers at your business meeting, they should be there for a reason. The reasons are usually one of the following:

1. He/she is a future minute taker

2. He/she is a graduate trainee, attending as part of their professional development

3. He/she is the chairperson's mentor

You may have a different reason for having observers at your meeting. Just ensure they aren't present for the sake of it. Note: observers should only attend the meeting if the chairperson has agreed to it.

Before the meeting:

1. Understand why you are attending the meeting. Never be frightened to ask why you have been invited to attend the meeting

2. Read the agenda and accompanying documents

During the meeting:

1. Observe but do not contribute to the meeting

2. Make notes if you have the chairperson's permission to do so

After the meeting:

1. Type any necessary notes

2. Give feedback to the chairperson (only if invited to do so)

3. Ask any questions you have

4. Do not discuss anything that was confidential in the meeting

Public meetings (e.g. company AGMs or shareholder meetings) often have large numbers of observers. There will be guidelines regarding who can and can't observe these meetings.

If members of the public or the press are present at the meeting they will be noted in the minutes. The number of observers generally makes it impractical to name each individual. Therefore, the minutes will simply reflect the number of observers. The minutes may separate 'public observers' from 'the press'.

Like any other business meeting, as an observer you won't be able to actively participate. Some people like to attend public company AGMs as a way of finding out the company's plans for the future.

I can't think of any circumstances that would require observers at informal meetings. Due to the nature of an informal meeting everyone is expected to contribute in some way.

# 7. Planning the Meeting

Never underestimate the value of proper planning and preparation for meetings. The chairperson will already have decided that a meeting is necessary or the best option. Next, consider who should attend, date, time and suitable meeting place.

Once this is sorted out it's time to work on the agenda. All of these are key elements of the planning stage of every meeting. Poor preparation leads to inefficient meetings. Whereas careful planning and a well thought out agenda can save time and achieve better results.

An agenda is a list or plan of the matters for discussion at the meeting. However it looks the agenda is an essential part of formal and business meetings. It's useful for informal meetings, although you could simply create a list of matters to be discussed.

Some people issue the agenda at the start of the meeting or, worse still, not at all. It's important to issue the agenda sufficiently far in advance to give all attendees time to prepare properly. The reasons for having an agenda and issuing it in advance are:

1. To ensure the meeting is an efficient use of company time and money

2. To ensure everyone knows what will be discussed at the meeting

3. To ensure everything important is dealt with during the meeting

4. To make sure only relevant topics are covered

5. It makes chairing the meeting easier as it provides a framework

6. It makes the minute takers role easier as he/she has headings for the notes

7. It gives structure to the meeting

8. It helps reduce meeting time

The time spent compiling the agenda will help ensure an efficient meeting. In short, it's worth the effort.

Spending time creating the right agenda will ensure that never again do you have irrelevant agenda items as part of your meeting. Little steps like this will make a big difference to the efficiency of your meeting.

**Handy hint:** Only include agenda items that are relevant to the majority of the attendees. Any item that only affects a small percentage of the attendees should be dealt with outside the meeting.

If your meeting involves sensitive or confidential items only issue the agenda to the regular attendees. As an added precaution, it might be helpful to alert the attendees to the confidential agenda items in a covering email. This isn't strictly necessary but it does help preserve the confidentiality of the meeting.

If you are planning an informal meeting you may decide that an agenda is not necessary. This is fine. It's still important to have a meeting plan or a brief list of topics for discussion though. This will ensure the meeting stays focused.

**Handy hint:** Never book more agenda items that the meeting can accommodate. Rushed meetings rarely cover the agenda items properly.

You may find it helpful create your own agenda template for future meetings. Agenda templates are available in Microsoft Word if you don't want to create your own template. To find a Microsoft template open a new Word document, select the 'File' tab. Then select 'New' and then 'Agendas'.

I prefer to create my own template. It's just as easy to do and means the document is tailored to your meetings.

**Handy hint:** If you issue the agenda at the start of the meeting or not at all participants won't have time to prepare. The meeting is likely to take longer and the discussions may not be as productive.

# 7.1 Obtaining Agenda Items

Always give a deadline for the receipt of agenda items and stick to it. Discourage late submissions by not accepting late agenda items, apart from in exceptional circumstances. Any agenda item that arrives after the cut-off date should be held back until the next meeting.

If the meeting is monthly or less frequent the cut-off date for agenda items is 8 working days before the meeting. For weekly meetings the cut-off date is 4 working days before the meeting.

When planning the agenda consider the length of the meeting. The meeting needs to be long enough to complete the business. Ideally meetings shouldn't be longer than two hours. People find it hard to maintain a good level of concentration after this time. Meetings lasting longer than two hours should include a short comfort break in the middle.

Don't feel you must include agenda items just because you have been asked to. The following are reasons **not** to include an agenda item:

1. The item isn't relevant to the meeting

2. It doesn't involve the majority of the attendees

3. It could be dealt with outside the meeting

If in doubt ask the chairperson whether he/she wishes to include the agenda item or not.

If the chairperson/meeting secretary decides to accept late agenda items treat them as 'Any other business'. Otherwise it will be necessary to reissue the agenda.

Each attendee should advise how much meeting time is required for their agenda item. You don't need to include timings on the agenda. However, the meeting secretary needs to know how long each agenda item requires for scheduling purposes. You can't accurately schedule meeting without this information.

Creating a good agenda is a skill. Next time you attend a meeting perhaps you will be aware of the effort that went into creating it.

## 7.2 Agenda Styles

There are three styles of agenda. These are:

1. Basic Agenda
2. Full Agenda
3. Objectives Agenda

The agenda is like any other business document. Regardless of the style of agenda you choose, it should be written in black and white. This is not the time to produce a creative work of art.

There are pros and cons associated with each style of agenda. I have provided details of each agenda style so you can choose the right one for your meetings.

**Basic Agenda**

The basic agenda is the most commonly used style of agenda for business meetings. This agenda style is suitable for most business meetings.

This style of agenda is popular as it's clean, simple and easy to compile. Most meeting secretaries are able to create this style of agenda without help from the chairperson or other attendees. This agenda is a good starting point for anyone new to creating agendas.

There is a downside to the basic agenda. The headings can sometimes be vague. This can lead to misunderstanding about what is going to be discussed under each heading.

If you use the basic agenda for your meetings the chairperson needs to be strong and disciplined. Otherwise attendees may use the generic headings to discuss a variety of topics, some of which are irrelevant to the meeting.

If you are going to use the basic agenda (most organisations do), then ensure the headings are clear and specific. This saves misunderstanding during the meeting. It might be helpful for the chairperson to introduce each agenda item with a quick summary.

Basic agendas are ideal for meetings where everyone understands the required outcomes. This style of agenda is also popular for report-back and project planning meetings.

Apart from 'Apologies' each item on the basic agenda should be numbered. This is necessary as the same numbering will appear on the minutes. Simply create a numbered list of all the topics for discussion.

Under 'Matters arising' list each outstanding action from the previous meeting, the action owner and reference number from the minutes.

**Full Agenda**

The full agenda is often used for formal meetings (e.g. board meetings, AGM's etc). The full agenda provides more detailed information than the basic agenda. It contains subheadings where there is more than one discussion point under a particular agenda item. For example:

**6. Personnel Matters**
6.1 Annual salary review
6.2 Training plans for the current financial year
6.3 The future use of temporary staff

Creating a full agenda creates more work for the meeting secretary. Although it takes more time and effort to create It's helpful to the people attending the meeting. If you're undecided about whether to use this style of agenda for your business meetings, weigh up the pros and cons.

A full agenda provides a clear idea of what will be discussed during the meeting. It also indicates who is leading each discussion (if anyone). This style of agenda is particularly helpful to inexperienced chairmen/women. It helps the chairperson to keep the meeting focused on what should be discussed.

There is a downside to the full agenda. The person creating the agenda is not always able to do so without help from the chairperson and/or attendees. Inexperienced meeting secretaries sometimes struggle with this style of agenda initially. It's also worth saying; most business meetings don't need this level of detail.

For this style of agenda the attendees should be very clear and concise when providing details of their agenda item. In as few words as possible each subheading should include what is to be discussed.

Introductions/welcome, Minutes of the previous meeting, Any other business and Date of next meeting are all main agenda headings. However, there are no subheadings for these agenda items.

**Objectives Agenda**
The objectives agenda is both lengthy and time consuming to produce.

The primary difference between an objectives agenda and a full agenda is the terminology used. The objectives agenda states what has to be achieved as a result of the discussion. The full agenda states what is to be discussed. For example '4.3 To update attendees on the Annual Housing Conference (HF)'.

The objectives agenda is no longer commonly used as it's wordy and cumbersome. It's also more difficult to create and adds little value to the meeting. Most organisations are now opting for the full agenda in place of the objectives agenda.

If you decide to use an objectives agenda here is a list of the objectives typically stated:

To receive…
To decide…
To discuss…
To agree…

To approve...
To establish...
To explore...
To select...
To review...
To confirm...

The objectives agenda contains subheadings where there is more than one discussion point under a particular agenda item. For example:

**6. Personnel Matters**
6.1 To discuss the annual salary review
6.2 To agree the training plans for the current financial year
6.3 To agree on the future use of temporary staff, or not

Attendees should be very clear and concise when providing details of their agenda item. In as few words as possible the subheading should indicate what the expected outcome of the discussion is.

Introductions/welcome, Minutes of the previous meeting, Any other business and Date of next meeting are all main agenda headings. However, there are no subheadings for these agenda items.

**Handy hint:** If you decide to use the objectives agenda it will be necessary to set aside three times longer for the agenda preparation, the meeting and writing the minutes.

It's normal for the minute taker to need help to write an objectives agenda. It requires detailed knowledge of the agenda items to write this agenda. It's better to seek help than to struggle and produce an inaccurate agenda on your own.

# 7.3 Agenda Layout

Regardless of which style of agenda you opt for every agenda should have a clear header that contains the following information:

Name of the group that is meeting

Date and start time of the meeting

Venue (full meeting address)

You can centre or left justify the header section of your agenda. This is a matter of personal choice. If it's any help, most organisations opt to centre the header section and left justify the rest of the document. I have left justified the header section in the examples I've created.

Leave at least two blank lines after the header section. The white space helps to make the document visually appealing and easy to read.

The heading 'Agenda' is generally centred. Leave at least two blank lines after the heading. Once again, this is to make the document easy to read.

Moving onto the main body of the document... decide whether you are going to use the basic, full or objectives agenda style. Whichever you choose, the same layout and numbering must be used for the agenda and the minutes.

Ideally, you should be aiming to get the entire agenda on a single A4 page. This isn't always possible for lengthy meetings with lots of matters to discuss. The length of your agenda will dictate the line spacing you use to separate the agenda items.

The order of agenda items is the same for each of the agenda styles. Present your agenda in the following order:

Apologies

Welcome, introductions and administration

Minutes of the previous meeting

Matters arising

Reports

Main agenda items

Any other business

Date of next meeting

All of this information forms part of the audit trail. An internal quality auditor should be able to easily match the two documents up during an audit inspection.

Currently the most popular fonts for business writing are Arial or Verdana. These are both clear, easy to read fonts, which makes them a popular choice. By varying the font size for different parts of the document you make it easier for the reader to spot what they are looking for. Here are my suggestions for your agenda document:

Name of the group or meeting - Arial 14 or 16 point bold text

Date and start time of the meeting - Arial 12 point bold text

Meeting venue - Arial 12 point bold text

Document title - Agenda - Arial 14 or 16 point bold text

Main headings - Arial 12 point bold text

Sub-headings (full and objectives agenda) - Arial 11 point bold text

Objectives description - Arial 11 point text (objectives agenda only)

# 7.4 Agenda Examples

I thought you might find it helpful to have an example of a basic agenda, full agenda and objectives agenda.

### Example of a Basic Agenda
Here is an example of the layout of a basic agenda.

**Name of the group that is meeting**
**Date and start time of the meeting**
**Venue (full meeting address)**

**Agenda**

Apologies

### 1. Welcome, introductions and administration

### 2. Minutes of the previous meeting

### 3. Matters arising
Maternity cover for Sukhi Patel (PC) 5.0
Replacement scheme manager for Redrock Place (SP) 6.0
Resolve anti-social behaviour issues with the tenant at 10 Parsons Lane (BE) 7.0

### 4. Reports
Finance Report (FF)
Company Risk Assessment (RP)

### 5. Official opening of the Sun Rising Village Development by Barrie Boulder MP

### 6. Training budget and plans for the current financial year

### 7. Purchase of additional land at Sun Rising Village (HH)

### 8. Any other business

### 9. Date of next meeting

### Example of a Full Agenda
As you will see from the example below, the full agenda is far more detailed than the basic agenda. It's important to include sub-headings for each discussion point.

**Name of the group that is meeting**
**Date and start time of the meeting**
**Venue (full meeting address)**

**Agenda**

**Apologies**

**1. Welcome, introductions and administration (or a variation on this)**

**2. Minutes of the previous meeting**

**3. Matters arising**
3.1 Maternity cover for Sukhi Patel (PC) 5.0
3.2 Replacement scheme manager for Redrock Place (SP) 6.3
3.3 Resolve anti-social behaviour issues with the tenant at 10 Parsons Lane (BE) 7.3

**4. Reports**
4.1 Finance Report (FF)
4.2 Company Risk Assessment (RP)

**5. Official opening of the Sun Rising Village Development by Barrie Boulder MP**
5.1 Timetable for visit (draft timetable attached) (WW)
5.2 Duties Barrie Boulder will perform (RC)
5.3 Publicity for the event (SS)
5.4 Security issues (TT)

**6. Training budget and plans for the current financial year**
6.1 Training budget (FF)
6.2 Agree essential training programmes
6.3 Mentors for graduate trainees

**7. Purchase of additional land at Sun Rising Village (HH)**
7.1 The likely cost of purchasing the land
7.2 The number and style of properties to be built
7.3 Financing the project (FF)
7.4 Timescale for completing the project

**8. Any other business**

**9. Date of next meeting**

**Example of an Objectives Agenda**
The objectives agenda isn't commonly used as it's wordy and cumbersome. Here is an example in case you want to create an objectives agenda for your meeting.

**Name of the group that is meeting**
**Date and start time of the meeting**
**Venue (full meeting address)**

## Agenda

Apologies

**1. Welcome, introductions and administration** (or a variation on this)
To welcome everyone to the meeting, make the introductions and deal with housekeeping matters

**2. Minutes of the previous meeting**
To review and adopt the minutes of the previous meeting

**3. Matters arising**
3.1 To provide an update on the maternity cover for Sukhi Patel (PC) 5.0
3.2 To appoint a replacement scheme manager for Redrock Place (SP) 6.3
3.3 To provide an update on the anti-social behaviour issues with the tenant at 10 Parsons Lane (BE) 7.3

**4. Reports**
4.1 To receive the finance report from FF
4.2 To receive the group's updated risk assessment from RC
4.3 To receive the training budget and plans for the current financial year report from MM

**5. Official opening of the Sun Rising Village Development by Barrie Boulder MP**
5.1 To finalise the timetable for visit (draft timetable attached) (WW)
5.2 To discuss the duties Barrie Boulder will perform (RC)
5.3 To agree the publicity for the event (SS)
5.4 To discuss the security issues (TT)

**6. Training budget and plans for the current financial year**
6.1 To agree the training budget (FF)
6.2 To agree what is essential training for the current financial year
6.3 To select the mentors for this year's intake of graduate trainees

**7. Purchase of additional land at Sun Rising Village (HH)**
7.1 To discuss the likely cost of purchasing the land and agree if this is financially viable
7.2 To agree the number and style of properties to be built
7.3 To agree how the project should be financed (FF)
7.4 To discuss the timescale for completing the project

**8. Any other business**
To discuss any urgent items presented under 'Any other business'

**9. Date of next meeting**
To agree the date for the next meeting

# 7.5 Agenda Headings Explained

Never allocate a number to 'Apologies' on your agenda. The numbering on the minutes must match the agenda numbering. This will not be possible if you make 'Apologies' number 1 on your agenda.

The heading 'Apologies' on the agenda is simply there as a reminder that people should notify their absence in advance.

## Welcome, Introductions and Administration
Welcome, introductions and administration are always item number 1 on the agenda. This housekeeping task can be beneficial to the overall efficiency of the meeting.

If the attendees don't know each other, it's common courtesy to introduce everybody. This agenda item also provides the chairperson with an opportunity to state any ground rules. Remember to ask everyone to switch off their mobile phones and other electronic devices.

This agenda item is used to state the purpose of the meeting, and any decisions that need to be taken. Doing this will help to get everyone focused on the task in hand.

Not all agendas include a heading for 'Welcome, introductions and administration'. This is generally the case for groups who meeting regularly. Some informal meetings don't include this agenda item.

I recommend this agenda item for every meeting. Although it only takes a couple of minutes the benefits can be far reaching.

## Minutes of the Previous Meeting
The purpose of 'this agenda item is to accept the minutes from the last meeting. This is the only opportunity to amend the minutes from the previous meeting.

**Handy hint:** Do not be tempted to amend the minutes between meetings. Anyone wishing to make a change to the minutes should wait until the next meeting.

**Matters Arising**

Matters arising are the actions from the previous meeting. These are sometimes listed as actions from the previous meeting. People often confuse 'Matters arising' with 'Minutes of the previous meeting'.

List each action from the previous meeting on the agenda. Include the initials of the person responsible for the action and the reference number from the previous meeting's minutes. This makes minute taking and internal auditing easier.

Each Matter arising needs to be sufficiently clear for the chairperson to prompt the action owner for the right information.

If any of the Matters arising relate to topics that will be covered under the main agenda items deal with it under the main agenda items. There is no point discussing it twice. 'Matters arising' is just for updating previous actions, not new discussions.

It's good practice for the meeting secretary to obtain an update for each action before the next meeting. This ensures the chairperson and minute taker already know what is going to be said. This can be minuted in advance. Providing an update during the meeting is for the benefit of the attendees.

Some organisations prefer to create a separate table of actions. This document is then referred to during the meeting, when dealing with Matters arising. This is a matter of personal choice.

If you want to create a 'Table of Actions' you will need to create a table with four columns. The headings are as follows:

Column one - Reference Number (from the previous minutes)

Column two - Details of the Action

Column three - Action Owner

Column four - Action Update

Some organisations issue this document with the agenda. Others just provide the chairperson and minute taker with a copy of the Table of Actions. This is a matter of personal choice.

**Handy hint:** Always include the initials of the action owner and reference number from the previous minutes on the agenda. This makes the chairperson's and minute taker's job easier.

## Reports

Reports and other documents should be issued with the agenda. Each attendee is expected to read the reports before the meeting. This improves the efficiency of the meeting and saves time.

On the agenda 'Reports' are dealt with after the Matters arising. Under the heading 'Reports' list each report that is not a matter for discussion at the meeting.

Any reports to be discussed during the meeting should be listed under the main agenda items, not the 'Reports' heading. This tells the attendees the report needs to be read in advance, but will be discussed during the meeting.

On the front page of the relevant report (or other document) write the agenda item number. This cross referencing helps ensure an efficient use of meeting time, and provides a clear audit trail.

You may not have any reports for your meetings. If you don't have any reports there is no need to include this heading on your agenda.

**Handy hint:** Always include the name or initials of the report owner on the agenda. This is helpful to the chairperson during the meeting.

## Main Agenda Items

It's the meeting secretary or chairperson's responsibility to decide the order of the main agenda items. Always list the urgent or most important items first. If the meeting overruns you will have dealt with the most important matters.

Try not to create an unduly long agenda. Unless you have set aside several hours you're unlikely to get through everything. Agenda items that are closely linked can be grouped together if it's practical to do so. For example, 'Personnel Matters' could encompass annual leave, salary reviews, recruitment or redundancy etc.

Alternatively, you may prefer to list each agenda item separately. It really is a matter of personal choice. The only rule is don't list more items than you can comfortably deal with in the time available.

One person may be leading the discussion for a particular agenda item. If so, put their name or initials next to the agenda item. If the topic is a free-for-all discussion don't put anyone's name next to the item on the agenda.

This is useful information for the chairperson during the meeting. The chairperson will know who is going to lead the discussion, or that the topic is for general debate.

This is another example of how to improve the efficiency of your meetings. The good news is it doesn't make any extra work for the meeting secretary. It only takes seconds to put someone's initials on the agenda.

**Handy hint:** Always list the main agenda items in order of importance. If your meeting runs out of time you can simply carry the less important matters forward to the next meeting.

### Any Other Business (AOB)
For the majority of your meetings there should be nothing to discuss under the heading of Any other business (AOB). This heading should always appear on the agenda though.

If everyone has submitted their agenda items on time there will be nothing to discuss when the meeting reaches this point. This is good news as most people have had enough by the time you reach Any other business.

Items for discussion under Any other business should only be **urgent** matters that came to light after the agenda was issued.

If there are any matters to discuss under Any other business they should be agreed with the chairperson before the meeting. On the chairperson's and minute taker's copy of the agenda add the details of these urgent items. Do not reissue the agenda to everyone else.

### Date of Next Meeting
This is a prompt for the chairperson to fix the date of the next meeting before concluding this one. This is the final matter to be dealt with before the chairperson formally closes the meeting.

## Exercise: Any Other Business

Any other business is the most misunderstood and abused part of any meeting. Spend a few moments thinking about the meetings you attend.

### Instructions:
Answer the following questions:

1. Do you often have anything to discuss under 'Any other business'?

2. What is normally discussed under Any other business in the meetings you attend?

3. Does the chairperson use 'Any other business' to ask everyone for their personal updates?

4. Are attendees invited to suggest topics when you reach 'Any other business', without the chairperson agreeing this advance?

# 7.6 The Chairperson's Agenda

This is sometimes known as the 'chairperson's brief'. The chairperson's agenda is a more detailed version of the document issued to everyone else. This document can be very helpful to the chairperson during the meeting.

The chairperson's agenda should include timings, highlights what is required from each agenda item and any other useful background information. Here are two examples of what might be included on the chairperson's agenda:

### 10.45   4. Staff for the new community office

Discuss the staffing level required for the new community office (All). Confirm the set up costs (FF)

Select a project owner to oversee the new office opening (All)

### 11.05   5. Maternity cover for Betty McBricker

Discuss plans for Betty McBricker's maternity cover. Are we going to recruit someone on a short-term contract or use agency staff to provide maternity cover? (BR)

We need to make a decision at this meeting as Betty McBricker will be leaving in 8 weeks' time

The chairperson's agenda can be as detailed as you wish. Some chairmen/women find it helpful to include the expected outcome for each agenda item. Typical outcomes include:

1. Decision
2. Discussion
3. Information
4. Planning (e.g. workshop sessions)
5. Generating ideas
6. Getting feedback

7. Finding solutions
8. Agreeing (targets, budgets, aims etc)
9. Policy statement
10. Team building/motivation
11. Guest speaker - information, initiatives etc

**Handy hint:** It's worth finding out how detailed each chairperson likes his/her agenda to be. This will enable you to create a tailor made agenda to suit their needs.

## Exercise: Creating and Using the Agenda

Hopefully you now appreciate the value of a good agenda. Think about the meetings you attend and the quality of the agenda. This includes agendas created by you and those created by others.

**Instructions:**

Answer the following questions.

1. Do your agendas always contain the essential information identified in this chapter? If not, what is missing?

2. Is every agenda written in a way that everyone can understand what is to be discussed?

3. During the meeting, does the chairperson stick to the order of the agenda? If not you might like to revise your agenda template

4. Do you have an agenda template that you adapt for all meetings? If not you might like to consider doing this as it will save preparation time in future

## Exercise: Create the Chairperson's Agenda

You have a meeting scheduled for one hour only, and you need to ensure that everything is dealt with in that time. Your brief is to create an agenda for the chairperson. You can choose the style of agenda you wish to use. There are no right or wrong answers to this exercise; it's a matter of personal choice.

The items on your agenda are:

1. Welcome
2. Minutes of the previous meeting
3. Matters arising

4. Reports - Finance Report and the Risk Assessment Register

5. Main agenda items. You have three main agenda items

6. Any other business

7. Date of the next meeting

**Instructions:**

1. Your meeting is scheduled from 10.30 - 11.30 am. Put the timings on the chairperson's agenda

2. You have four Matters arising from the previous meeting. You need to allow sufficient time for the chairperson and each action owner to speak. This part of the meeting shouldn't take up most of the meeting time

3. You plan to remove two items from the risk assessment register. You need to allow time for a short discussion before these items are removed. This agenda item shouldn't take as long as the main agenda items

4. You have three main agenda items to discuss. How long are you going to allow for each one? Note: you don't have to allocate the same amount of time to each one

5. There is nothing to discuss under 'Any other business'

6. The chairperson needs to fix the date for the next meeting

7. How did you get on? Did you manage to allocate enough time to each agenda item, and complete the agenda in one hour?

# 8. Getting Prepared for the Meeting

The minute taker is often asked to be the meeting secretary as well. This involves organising the meeting. It may include booking the meeting room, booking parking spaces and ordering refreshments (if appropriate). It also involves inviting agenda items, producing and issuing the agenda, reports and other documents.

Meetings fall into two categories - regular meetings (any group that meets more than once) and the one-off meeting. It's important to understand which category of meeting you are planning, as the organisation of it may vary. For a one-off meeting it's helpful to explain to each participant why he/she needs to attend.

If an internal meeting is anything more than a one-to-one with a colleague you really should consider recording the meeting. This involves formal minutes or informal meeting notes.

If the meeting is a regular one it's good practice to arrange the next meeting date before concluding the current meeting. It's much easier to agree a meeting date when everyone is together.

If a meeting has to be rescheduled after the date has been fixed find out who the essential attendees are. Agree the meeting date with these 'essential' attendees. Some non-essential attendees may not be able to attend the meeting but this will have minimal impact on the meeting.

It's difficult to agree a mutually convenient date if all attendees are not together when the date is being canvassed. This is why you focus on the availability of the essential attendees only.

## 8.1 Dealing With Visitors

Being a visitor at a meeting can feel quite daunting as you are the outsider amongst a group that meets regularly. The chairperson and meeting secretary can make the experience a positive one. Make sure visitors clearly understand what is expected of them.

If your meeting involves visitors let them know if they need to attend the entire meeting. If not tell them what time they need to arrive. Also make it clear how long they are likely to be at the meeting. This helps visitors to schedule their time.

If a visitor is delivering a presentation at the meeting obtain a copy of the presentation or notes. Attach this to the minutes. Also ensure any equipment needed for the visitor's agenda item is booked (e.g. laptop projector for PowerPoint presentations etc). Ask your visitors if there if they require any other assistance.

**Handy hint:** Ask visitors to provide a copy of their presentation, notes or reference material in advance. This is one thing less to think about during the meeting.

## 8.2 Dealing With Apologies

Apologies can be received at any time before the meeting. It's common for people to offer their apologies when the next meeting date is being canvassed. Alternatively this may happen in advance of the meeting and sometimes via another attendee at the meeting. Whenever and however the apologies are received it's important that you record the apologies in the minutes.

When accepting apologies from a attendee ensure they provide an update for their actions from the previous meeting. If the attendee has not provided an update the chairperson won't be able to deal with the action during the meeting. In this case the relevant action will need to be carried forward to the next meeting. This is not efficient and creates a messy audit trail.

## 8.3 Meeting Checklist

When planning a meeting it's useful to have a checklist. This ensures nothing gets forgotten. A good meeting checklist includes all the tasks to be completed before the meeting, and everything that is needed during the meeting. Simply tick tasks off as you complete them.

**Handy hint:** Laminate your meeting checklist and use a marker pen to write on it. This will provide a wipe-clean surface, saving you the need to produce a new checklist for each meeting.

## 8.4 Preparing the Minute Taker's Notepad

Before the meeting starts ensure your notepad is already prepared. This will save time and make the task of note taking more efficient. An A4 pad is absolutely ideal for note taking. Simply divide your notepad into four columns and write the following headings:

Column 1 - Lead (this column can be narrow as it's just for the initials of the person leading the discussion. This is in case of query)

Column 2 - Notes/Actions (make this the widest column as it will have most information)

Column 3 - Action Owner and Completion Date (this column can be fairly narrow as it will only have very limited information)

Column 4 - Extra Notes (this column is just in case the anything extra is added to this agenda item later in the meeting. Hopefully this column should rarely be used)

The other task you might like to do before the meeting starts is write a list of the names of all attendees. Next to their name write their initials. During the meeting just use the initials to identify people.

## 8.5 Chairperson/Minute Taker Briefing Session

It's good practice for the chairperson and minute taker to have a short pre-meeting. The day before the meeting is ideal for this. When I say this at workshops and seminars I'm often confronted with blank faces.

This essential task is often ignored or dismissed by chairmen/women as a waste of time. How wrong!

## Exercise: Chairperson/Minute Taker Briefing Session

If you chair meetings answer these four short questions.

1. As the chairperson do you always arrange a short briefing with your minute taker?

2. If not, why not?

3. Do you understand the purpose and value of this briefing?

4. Will you be arranging a chairperson/minute taker briefing in future?

If you don't currently have a chairperson/minute taker briefing I hope I can persuade you of the value of this:

1. The purpose of this meeting is to discuss the content of the meeting. Specifically it's about any help either of you might need during the meeting

2. Does the chairperson need help managing the timings? It's easy to get caught up in the discussions and find precious time being gobbled up

3. Does the minute taker know what needs to be minuted or does he/she need to be told what to minute?

4. Does the chairperson have a strategy for dealing with awkward or challenging attendees?

5. Are there any contentious topics on the agenda? How is this going to be handled?

6. Is there likely to be anything discussed that shouldn't be minuted?

In the time it takes to drink a cup of coffee all of this can be discussed. Just 10 minutes spent having this discussion in advance could significantly improve the quality of the meeting.

If you don't already do this I challenge you to try it and see if it makes a difference to your meetings.

# 9. The Meeting

According to psychologists the way a meeting starts sets the tone for the whole meeting. If the meeting starts with complaints, problems or blame, you can expect more of the same. This is unlikely to result in the most productive meeting.

It's important to know that during the meeting the minute taker is deemed to be part of the management team. This rule applies even if the minute taker is a junior member of staff. The role of minute taker is hugely important and often underestimated.

## 9.1 Note Taking and Recording Actions

The minute taker's role starts as soon as the chairperson opens the meeting. While the chairperson is dealing with the housekeeping matters the minute taker should be making a note of all attendees. It's also important to make a note of who is absent. It's essential that you have an accurate record of who was present and who was absent.

There is generally no need to capture everything that is said during the meeting. If the chairperson wants a record of everything that is said he/she should make this clear before the meeting starts.

It's normal to have duplication and surplus notes from the meeting. Don't worry about this during the meeting; simply edit the notes afterwards. The most important information to capture is details of all the actions, action owners and completion dates. It's useful to have a summary of the discussion that took place, but these don't need to be detailed notes.

If you are using the full or objectives agenda for your meeting you will need to summarise every discussion point. This means sub-headings as well as the main headings. The minutes relating to a full or objectives agenda are often lengthy, but this is unavoidable.

It's likely that the notes taken during the meeting will include personal comments, opinions, bias etc. None of these should appear in the minutes that are produced though. Be aware that sometimes meetings involve particularly important or controversial decisions. You may like to ask the chairperson to confirm what he/she wants minuted in these instances.

If you don't understand something that needs to be minuted interrupt and ask for clarification. It's much easier to do this during the meeting than afterwards.

No matter how carefully planned sometimes discussions go back to an agenda item already dealt with. If you have an 'extra notes' column in your notepad you can slot any additional comments in.

Otherwise you will have to write the extra notes in your notepad with a note explaining which agenda item it relates to. This is time consuming, and may mean you miss something important.

**Handy hint:** Good meeting notes include the speaker, a summary of the discussion, details of actions, action owner and completion date. The speaker won't appear in the minutes but it's useful to have this information in case of query.

There are a few useful rules regarding note taking in meetings. Here are the nine things you should be aware of:

1. Make as many notes as you feel you need. Remember we're all different so no two people will take the same amount of notes

2. Write bullet points; you don't have time to write full sentences

3. Make a note of who is leading the discussion or making relevant comments. This is just in case of query after the meeting

4. Capture the message of the discussion, not a word-for-word account. The only exception is meetings where you've been asked to capture everything word-for-word

5. If the chairperson forgets to confirm the action completion date, remind him/her before the meeting moves on. Action owners can't be chased if no completion date has been agreed

6. Identify the agenda item your notes relate to. It's harder to do this after the meeting

7. Confirm names, jargon etc you don't understand. It's better to ask than issue incorrect minutes

8. If an argument ensues at the meeting take care not to capture the emotion. Only record the discussion, as you would normally

9. At all times keep the Freedom of Information Act in mind. This is particularly important if there is any possibility of your minutes being read by anyone outside the organisation

Keep a copy of the agenda in front of you during the meeting. You will probably need to refer to it frequently throughout the meeting.

Actions can only be allocated to someone present at the meeting as there is no mechanism for reporting the outcome otherwise. The action owner may choose to delegate the task to someone who didn't attend the meeting.

This is fine. As far as the minutes are concerned the action owner remains the person assigned during the meeting. He/she will be responsible for ensuring the action is completed and providing an update at the next meeting.

The person completing the action isn't automatically entitled to a copy of the minutes. It's the action owner's responsibility to share the details of the action with the person who will do the work.

If there are no actions from a particular discussion summarise the discussion in the usual way. Add a note stating that there were no actions from the agenda item. This will be helpful to anyone reading the minutes at a later date.

When agreeing the actions for each agenda item make sure there is an action owner and completion date. It's important that everyone understands what they are expected to do and when. Without an action owner and completion date it will be difficult to make anyone accountable for their actions. This may result in actions not being completed before the next meeting.

**Handy hint:** Don't allow the meeting to move forward until the action owner and completion date have been agreed. You will struggle to sort this out after the meeting.

## Exercise: Note Taking Exercise

The purpose of this exercise is to give you experience of taking notes during a meeting. Unless you are a shorthand secretary or speedwriter you will find it virtually impossible to capture everything that is said.

A lot of the discussions in meetings aren't sufficiently important to capture. Note taking during meetings is about capturing the essential information for the minutes.

During our fictitious meeting the group discussed four main agenda items. We have included quite a bit of information about these discussions. Your task is to decide what you need to write in your notes. There are no right or wrong answers to this exercise.

**Instructions:**

1. Read the text below and get a good understanding of it. You may need to read it more than once before writing your notes

2. If you were in this meeting what notes would you make for each of these agenda items? Write your notes down on a sheet of paper

3. Now you've created your notes convert them into summary minutes. Each summary should be no more than three or four sentences long

4. Now identify the actions and action owners

**Discussion Points:**

**Official opening of the Sandblast Development** – a very lengthy discussion took place regarding the opening of the Sandblast development by Barrie Boulder MP.

Everyone had something to say on the subject but four of the group made a significant contribution to the discussion. Some of the group are unhappy that we are using Barrie Boulder as he's not a popular MP.

We're using him because we can't find any other high profile figure who is willing to do the opening free of charge. The discussion involved the timetable for the visit, the duties that Barrie Boulder will perform, publicity for the event and the security issues regarding the visit.

You should decide what the actions are, action owners and timescale.

**Refurbishment of the Bedrock Street flats** – The group discussed refurbishing the flats at Bedrock Street by providing new kitchens and bathrooms to all householders. The work will have to be completed with the residents' in-situ.

A budget of £2 million has been aside for the work, the successful contractors need to be notified and instructed to start work by the end of May, and all work must be finished by the end of the current financial year. We do not want this expenditure carrying over to the next financial year.

A project manager has been appointed and has been tasked with setting up the project and providing an update at the next meeting. Decide who the project manager is, what his/her initial tasks are when they must be completed by.

**Land for sale at Redrock** – The group discussed whether or not the organisation should purchase the land that's for sale at Redrock. This land would enable us to significantly increase our housing stock. This would be good news for us as demand is outstripping the housing stock available.

The group also discussed whether the development should be houses or flats. Freddie Fiscal has been asked to find out how much the land is going to cost. He's asked for a volunteer to assess how much it will cost to develop the site and whether it is likely to be affordable or not. You can decide who will have this action.

**Maternity Cover for Betty McBricker** - The group discussed providing maternity cover for Betty McBricker when she goes on maternity leave at the end of next month. The group spent a long time debating whether to recruit someone on a temporary contract or to simply use temporary staff from a local agency.

In the end the group decided to offer this role as a 12 month contract. One of the group needs to liaise with HR, write and advertise the vacancy. Decide what the actions are and who the action owner is going to be.

## 9.2 Other Ways to Record Minutes

There are other ways to record meetings. Personally, I believe minute taking is still the most effective method of providing an accurate record of a meeting. I'll leave you to make up your own mind once you have considered the following.

If the chairperson decides to record your meetings it's important to obtain the express permission of everyone present. It's not acceptable to just assume the consent is given just because people have attended the meeting.

### Recording Meetings
In this high-tech age it may seem logical to use electronic recording equipment to record your meeting. With good quality recording equipment and a very disciplined group, recording your meeting is a viable option.

In reality, most meetings involve more than one person speaking at once. The recording equipment will pick up every voice and other noise (e.g. clattering tea cups). Anyone listening to the recording after the meeting may struggle to follow the discussion. This may render the recording valueless.

If for any reason the electronic equipment fails you will have no record and no audit trail for the meeting. If you are happy to risk not having a record of your meeting this is fine.

If you need to have an accurate record of the meeting record the meeting and have a minute taker.

## Using a Laptop Computer

Using a laptop computer might seem like a good idea as you can type as you go, and so save time producing the minutes after the meeting. It's true that many of us can type faster than we write. However, before rushing for the laptop, consider the following:

Discussions often drift backwards and forwards. You will need to type the notes as the conversation drifts backwards and forwards. At the end of the meeting you will need to cut and paste the information into the correct part of the document. You won't have time search the relevant part of the document during the meeting.

If you opt to type your notes in the meeting you will end up with far more notes than necessary. Be prepared to delete a large chunk of the notes you create. Editing often takes longer than starting from scratch.

If you are going to type the minutes during the meeting save a copy of the document before you start cutting and pasting after the meeting.

You might like to arrange for someone to take written notes as a back-up plan. It's very easy to accidentally delete or lose a document and then have no record at all of the meeting.

## Apps

I couldn't write a book about meetings and minute taking without including something on apps. Nowadays there really is an app for everything in business, including minute taking. With so many apps to sift through, it can be hard to separate the useful from the gimmicky.

My initial intention was to do the research for you, but then I realised this is an impossible task. There are so many business apps available now that I would end up writing an entire book on the subject. Therefore, I shall leave you to do your own research.

Some traditionalists feel there is no room for apps in meetings. Others believe apps are the way forward and we should all embrace them wholeheartedly. Personally, I feel that we are all individual and should choose the option that works best for us.

You might like to try some apps and see how you get on. In your chosen search engine type the details of what you want the app to do. For example - type "apps for creating agendas for meetings". You can repeat this exercise for any aspect of your meeting.

## Exercise: Ways of Recording Minutes and Actions

Do you currently use the traditional method of recording the minutes and actions? Or, do you use technology to record your meetings? Before you go any further you might like to reflect on the best solution for your organisation going forward.

There are no right or wrong answers to this exercise. These are just your personal observations.

**Instructions:**

Consider the following.

1. How do you currently record the minutes and actions from your meetings?

2. Have you ever experienced technology failure and ended up with no minutes from the meeting? If not, you might like to have a strategy in mind for this eventuality

3. Have you used or considered minute taking apps? Is this something you're going to investigate for future meetings?

4. Are there any efficiencies you can make to the way minutes and actions are recorded in your meetings? If so, what are these?

5. Create an action plan for any changes you plan to make

# 10. Virtual Meetings

In these tough economic times organisations are constantly looking for cost savings and efficiencies. Everyone appreciates that meetings are expensive so virtual meetings seem like a no brainer. Technology makes it possible to get and view information without paper, which clearly provides cost savings.

Asking if virtual meetings will eventually replace all live meetings is like asking if online dating will eventually replace face-to-face dating. Clearly there is a role for virtual meetings but I believe there will always be a place for face-to-face meetings too.

Human face-to-face interaction is still the most effective form of communication. Live meetings deliver motivation, inspiration and messaging that even video conferencing can't quite match.

In my research for this chapter I discovered there is no consistent language when referring to virtual meetings. This just adds to the confusion. Should you have a webinar, webcast, WebEx, web meeting, virtual event, teleconference or videoconference? Confused? I was!

I've discovered what one organisation calls a virtual meeting another calls a webinar. What's more, calling a web presentation/meeting a WebEx is like describing all tissues as Kleenex. It's just a brand name.

I thought it might be helpful to find some common language. So, here goes:

Webinar - is a combination of web (online computer) and seminar. Webinars are really a web delivered lecture or training session. Webinars can be interactive events but the interaction comes from attendees typing their questions for the speaker. This isn't a good option for meetings but it's fine for presentations.

Webcast - is also a presentation that is delivered over the web. These are less interactive than webinars. Although fine for online presentations, a webcast doesn't work for meetings.

Web meetings - as the name suggests, these are meetings held on the web. They enable two-way communication. This can be audio only or audio and video. Web meetings seem to work best with small groups who want to share information or brainstorm.

Teleconferencing - as you would expect, this is an audio only meeting. Although we've been making telephone calls to each other for many years, teleconferencing is not a popular choice these days. Research suggests the message isn't always conveyed/received accurately, and concentration isn't as good. It's too easy to check your emails etc.

Videoconferencing - relies on visual and audio contact between the parties. Technology has moved on in leaps and bounds. Initially we were presented with grainy images and sometimes unclear audio transmission. However, now we can expect a high level of clarity.

Opinion is clearly still divided on the viability of virtual meetings. If it comes down to cost, virtual meetings may win on cost per meeting. However, there may be significant upfront costs, depending on the product you choose. Some people believe it's worth the cost of face-to-face meetings as the output is often better.

Before you rush off to cancel every face-to-face meeting you should weigh up the pros and cons of virtual meetings. You may come up with other pros or cons that I haven't listed. Here are some suggestions to get you started:

**Pros for Virtual Meetings**
- Cost per meeting
- Length of time everyone will be away from their desk
- You can involve people in multiple locations
- No travel time/cost involved
- Quick and efficient to set up if you have staff who are used to playing video games

**Cons for Virtual Meetings**
- The upfront cost may be significant. You will need to use the equipment regularly to make it a good investment
- It's harder to control a virtual meeting and the attendees
- Someone in each location has to know how to use the equipment
- You need to book a meeting room at each venue. There may be a cost for hiring meeting rooms
- They are not as effective as face-to-face meetings
- If people dislike virtual meetings or struggle with the technology they will be less motivated to attend
- Unless everyone logs in early the meeting won't start on time

If you decide to run a virtual meeting, here are the six factors that make a good virtual meeting:

1. You need to ensure everyone arrives in plenty of time. It takes time to get the equipment set up and running. You can't simply rush in at the appointed time and hey presto, off you go

2. Stay focused. This applies equally to the chairperson and the attendees. Short meetings work best as people have limited capacity to maintain concentration in virtual meetings

3. Establish some good meeting etiquette. It's much easier to start answering emails and text messages in a virtual meeting. This needs to be addressed as part of your ground rules. Agree all mobile phones will be switched off and no-one will access their emails during the meeting

4. In a virtual meeting it's even more important to ensure that everyone participates in the discussion. It would be easy to lose those who don't say anything

5. Provide some guidance or training on virtual meetings before introducing them into your organisation. Virtual meetings are a very different meeting experience. Each person who is expected to chair a virtual meeting needs to feel comfortable using the equipment. Otherwise you won't have a successful meeting

6. It's helpful for the chairperson and minute taker to be in the same room. Without this the chairperson won't know if the minute taker is struggling. Too often minute takers struggle in silence. In a virtual meeting the minute taker won't know who was taking comprehensive notes and can fill in the gaps

Other things to consider... According to researchers our brain has to work harder during a virtual meeting. This type of meeting poses some additional challenges for attendees. These include:

- Identifying who is speaking
- Coordinating eye contact
- Trying to take it in turn to speak
- Greater self-awareness, which often results in people saying less than in face-to-face meetings
- Being more judgemental about the speaker (i.e. liking or not liking the speaker)
- More influenced by likeability than quality of what is being said

In summary, virtual meetings can have a useful part to play in the 21st Century. However, they are highly unlikely to replace face-to-face meetings. I think it's a matter for you to decide how valuable, or not, virtual meetings will be in your organisation.

Finally, I have deliberately not suggested any brands or products for your virtual meetings. Technology is constantly changing. What is current today may well be out of date in 12 months' time. Therefore, I will leave you to do your own research on the right video conferencing equipment for your business/organisation.

## Exercise: Virtual Meetings

Are virtual meetings a part of your organisation currently? Before you go any further you might like to reflect on the potential role of virtual meetings going forward. There are no right or wrong answers to this exercise. These are just your personal observations.

**Instructions:**

Consider the following questions.

1. What type of virtual meetings have you attended?

2. What is your experience of virtual meetings? Weigh up the pros and cons in your experience

3. Do you see a role for virtual meetings in the future? If so, how are you going to make them work for all attendees?

4. If virtual meetings are already a part of your organisation, is everyone adequately trained? If not, how do you plan to address this?

# 11. The Minutes

The minutes are not a stand-alone document. The minutes need to mirror the agenda document in style, presentation and content.

Minutes are a valuable part of meetings. They provide an accurate record of the business of the meeting, are used to record actions, and identify the action owner. Most people have limited interest in the minutes. It's important to make sure they are well presented and easy to read.

Many organisations have no rules regarding minutes and offer very little guidance. How do you know whether you should be typing summary, verbatim or action point minutes? By understanding each type of minutes you will be able to suggest the best option for your organisation or meeting.

Formal and business meetings always have minutes. You may choose not to create minutes for an informal meeting but you should still have some notes from the meeting. Otherwise you have no record of what was discussed or agreed.

**Handy hint:** It's important that your minutes are written in plain English. You will find lots of really useful information on the Plain English Campaign website. The website address is - www.plainenglish.co.uk

## 11.1 Styles of Minutes

There are three styles of minutes. These are summary, verbatim and action point minutes. In theory any style of agenda can be used with any style of minutes. It's highly unlikely that you will ever find a full agenda or an objectives agenda being used with action point minutes.

It's important to know your organisation's preferred style of minutes. If there is no policy you or the chairperson can choose the style that you feel most comfortable with. Note: for most business meetings summary minutes are the preferred option.

### Summary Minutes
Summary minutes are the most commonly used style of minutes. They provide more information than action point minutes but less than verbatim minutes. Summary minutes capture the essential information, but as briefly as possible. This style of minutes is suitable for most business meetings.

Summary minutes follow the headings and numbering of the agenda (basic, full or objectives agenda). If the minutes are being used with a basic agenda, the summary can be presented however the minute taker wishes. Try to limit the summary to a maximum of five sentences.

If used with a full or objectives agenda the summary should follow the order of the sub-headings on the agenda. This will ensure the minutes tie up with the agenda accurately.

Prior to the meeting, the chairperson and minute taker should agree the level of detail for the minutes. This may help the minute taker to decide how many notes they need to take during the meeting.

**Verbatim Minutes**
In this case verbatim does not automatically mean word-for-word. Generally, it means everything that was discussed during the meeting. If the chairman/woman wants a word-for-word record of the meeting he/she should state this at the start of the meeting.

Verbatim minutes are often used for disciplinary hearings or meetings following a health and safety incident.

Verbatim minutes can make the task of minute taking challenging; especially if the discussion drifts backwards and forwards. This style of minutes requires a very disciplined chairperson who can keep the discussions focused and moving forwards.

Allow at least 70% more time to create verbatim minutes. Expect a very lengthy set of minutes if you are creating verbatim minutes with the full or objectives agenda.

**Action Point Minutes**
These are hardly minutes at all. This style of minutes comprises the headings from the agenda followed by the action, action owner and completion date.

Action point minutes are only really used for informal meetings or project meetings where you meet daily/weekly and just require an update. Most organisations feel these minutes provide insufficient information for business meetings.

Regardless of the style of minutes, if you have an agenda item without any actions indicate that there are no actions. This ensures you have an accurate audit trail for the meeting.

## 11.2 Layout of the Minutes

By varying the font size for different parts of the document you make it easier for the reader to spot what they are looking for. Here are my suggestions for your minutes document:

Name of the group or meeting - Arial 14 or 16 point bold text

Date and start time of the meeting - Arial 12 point bold text

Venue - Arial 12 point bold text

Document title - Minutes of [group/meeting name] - Arial 14 or 16 point bold text

Main headings - Arial 12 point bold text

Sub-headings (full and objectives agenda) - Arial 11 point bold text

Notes that makes up the minutes - Arial 11 point text

Details of actions - Arial 11 point italic text

Name of the action owner - Arial 10 point bold text

Completion date for actions - Arial 10 point text

All minutes, regardless of style, should have a header and the same numbering/headings as the agenda. This information makes it easy to audit both documents in future.

It's not necessary to include the finish time of your meeting, although some chairmen/women like to do so. Ask the chairperson if they want to include the finish time.

The header section of your minutes document should contain the following information:

Name of the group that is meeting

Date and start time of the meeting

Venue (full meeting address)

Leave at least two blank lines after the header section. The white space helps to make the document visually appealing and easy to read.

If you centred the header on your agenda document you should do the same thing for the minutes. Equally, if you left justified the header section (as per the example above) on your agenda document then this is how the header for your minutes document should appear.

Underneath the header section you should identify who was present and who was absent from the meeting. This information is not numbered, as it wasn't numbered on the agenda. Numbering this information would make the numbering of the two documents out of sync. Present and absent should be recorded as follows:

Present: The chairperson should be listed first, followed by the minute taker. After this it's a matter of personal choice how you list the attendees. The simplest way to do this is to list everyone present in alphabetical order by last name. Note: if you randomly list attendees you will find the person at the bottom of the list often takes offence as they think this makes them less important.

**Handy hint:** If you have a lot of attendees for your meeting you may like to list them in two columns to use less space

**Apologies:**

**Absent:** It's important to identify these people separately as you need an accurate record for audit purposes.

**Observers:** Most business meetings won't have observers. If you don't have any observers at your meeting don't bother with this heading.

Strictly speaking, you don't need to name observers as they haven't contributed to the meeting. You may choose to name the observer. In the case of public meetings e.g. AGM's there are often too many observers to name them. In which case write observers and the total number of observers.

If you have members of the press present at your meeting they should be recorded separately to the other observers. In this case after 'Observers' write another heading for 'Press' and the number or journalists present. Once again, they are not named in the minutes.

**Handy hint:** No one likes to be identified as 'Absent'. If some attendees are poor at sending their apologies and simply don't turn up for meetings this might stop this behaviour pattern.

Formal meetings are treated slightly differently. If you have non-board members present at the meeting, most organisations like to list these attendees under a separate heading of 'In attendance'.

If anyone attended the meeting for a single agenda item make a note of this. The simplest way to record this is to write the person's name and the agenda item in brackets. Although this may seem pedantic it does ensure you have an accurate record of your meeting for audit purposes.

Find out whether your chairman/woman wants to include the finish time of the meeting in the minutes.

## 11.3 Examples of Minutes Documents

Below is a typical example of how those present and absent might appear in your minutes. This part of the document will be the same whether you chose a basic, full or objectives agenda.

### Minutes of the [group name] meeting
#### Held on [date and start time of the meeting]
#### At [meeting address]

Present:
[Name] Chairperson
[Name] Minute taker
[Name] List the attendees in alphabetical order by last name
[Name]

Apologies:
[Name] List these in alphabetical order by last name
[Name]

Absent:
[Name] List these in alphabetical order by last name
[Name]

Leave at least two blank lines after this information. The white space helps to make the document visually appealing and easy to read.

The layout of the rest of the document should match the style and numbering you used in the agenda document. Below I have included examples of how the rest of your minutes document might look.

Personally, I think it's important to make the actions stand out from the minutes. This helps the action owners easily identify their actions. It also makes it easier for the meeting secretary when getting updates on outstanding actions.

White space on your document is important as it makes the minutes easier to read. Before anyone reads the content of the minutes they will do a visual check first. If the document doesn't look visually appealing the reader is likely to just scan, rather than read, the document.

**Example of Minutes Using a Basic Agenda**

Here is an example of the layout of the minutes when used with a basic agenda.

## 1. Welcome, introductions and administration
Summary of anything the chairperson wants minuted

## 2. Minutes of the previous meeting
The minutes of the meeting held on [date of the meeting] were approved

## 3. Matters arising
Maternity cover for Sukhi Patel - Summary.
Replacement scheme manager for Redrock Place – Summary
Resolve anti-social behaviour issues with the tenant at 10 Parsons Lane - Summary

## 4. Reports
Attach a copy of the reports to the minutes. This means you don't need to create a summary of each report. Just minute any comments made during the meeting. For completeness you may choose to add a note that says a copy of the reports are attached.
Finance Report
Company Risk Assessment

## 5. Official opening of the Sun Rising Village Development by Barrie Boulder MP
Summary
*Details of the actions*
**Action owner(s)** Completion date

## 6. Any other business

## 7. Date of next meeting
Date and time agreed for the next meeting

## Example of Minutes Using a Full Agenda
Here is an example of the layout of the minutes when used with a full agenda.

## 1. Welcome, introductions and administration (or a variation on this)
Summary of anything the chairperson wants minuted

## 2. Minutes of the previous meeting
The minutes of the meeting held on [date of the meeting] were approved

## 3. Matters arising
3.1 Maternity cover for Sukhi Patel - Summary
3.2 Replacement scheme manager for Redrock Place – Summary

3.3 Resolve anti-social behaviour issues with the tenant at 10 Parsons Lane - Summary

## 4. Reports

Attach a copy of the reports to the minutes. This means you don't need to create a summary of each report. Just minute any comments made during the meeting. For completeness you may choose to add a note that says a copy of the reports are attached.

4.1 Finance Report - Comments

4.2 Company Risk Assessment - Comments

## 5. Official opening of the Sun Rising Village Development by Barrie Boulder MP

5.1 Timetable for visit

Summary

*Details of the action*

**Action owner** Completion date

5.2 Duties Barrie Boulder will perform

Summary

*Details of the action*

**Action owner** Completion date

5.3 Publicity for the event

Summary

*Details of the action*

**Action owner** Completion date

5.4 Security issues

Summary

*Details of the action*

**Action owner** Completion date

## 6. Any other business

## 7. Date of next meeting

Date and time agreed for the next meeting

## Example of Minutes Using an Objectives Agenda

Here is an example of the layout of the minutes when used with an objectives agenda.

## 1. Welcome, introductions and administration (or a variation on this)

Summary of anything the chairperson wants minuted

## 2. Minutes of the previous meeting

The minutes of the meeting held on [date of the meeting] were approved

## 3. Matters arising
3.1 To provide an update on the maternity cover for Sukhi Patel - Summary

3.2 To appoint a replacement scheme manager for Redrock Place – Summary

3.3 To provide an update on the anti-social behaviour issues with the tenant at 10 Parsons Lane - Summary

## 4. Reports
Attach a copy of the reports to the minutes. This means you don't need to create a summary of each report. Just minute any comments made during the meeting. For completeness you may choose to add a note that says a copy of the reports are attached.

4.1 To receive the finance report from FF - Comments

4.2 To receive the group's updated risk assessment from RC - Comments

## 5. Official opening of the Sun Rising Village Development by Barrie Boulder MP
5.1 To finalise the timetable for visit
Summary
*Details of the actions*
**Action owner** Completion date

5.2 To discuss the duties Barrie Boulder will perform
Summary
*Details of the actions*
**Action owner** Completion date

5.3 To agree the publicity for the event
Summary
*Details of the actions*
**Action owner** Completion date

5.4 To discuss the security issues
Summary
*Details of the actions*
**Action owner** Completion date

## 6. Any other business

## 7. Date of next meeting
Date and time agreed for the next meeting

# Exercise: Create a Minutes Template

The document header section and the numbering must match on the agenda and the minutes. This forms part of the audit trail.

The order of the minutes must also match the order of the agenda (even if the meeting didn't follow this order. If you used a basic agenda then the numbering on the minutes must be the same. Equally, if you used a full or objectives agenda for your meeting the numbering on the minutes will include sub-headings.

**Instructions:**

1. Create a minutes template document that you can adapt for all your future meetings

2. Save a blank copy of this document as your master template

# 11.4 Creating the Minutes

So you're faced with pages and pages of notes and now need to convert these into clear, concise and accurate minutes. This task may seem daunting initially, but it's not as difficult as it first appears.

When creating the minutes there are a few rules. If you bear these in mind you will find the task easier:

1. The minutes must be a factual record of the discussion. This is not an opportunity to use your personal writing style

2. Keep the sentences as short (less than 20 words) and clear as possible

3. Write the minutes in the third person. There should be no reference to 'I, we, you, or your'

4. Don't include comments made by group members. If someone makes a specific comment during the meeting don't name them in the minutes

5. Keep the minutes succinct but without leaving important information out. Minute taking will develop your précis skills

There are some common phrases that often appear in minutes. Here are some typical examples to get you started. You don't need to use these examples they are just a starting point to help you when creating your minutes.

The meeting agreed that...

The meeting decided to...
The meeting resolved...
It was proposed that...
The meeting discussed...
The chairperson, finance director etc outlined new proposals for...
The marketing team will...
The chairperson suggested that...
A meeting is to be arranged to...
The chairperson informed the meeting that...
It was agreed that...
Concerns were expressed that...

If no decision was reached regarding an agenda item, record this in the minutes. For example 'no decision was reached'. This should be followed by a note that explains what happens next. For example - a sub-group will be set up to discuss the matter and come up with a proposal. This will be presented at the next meeting.

The numbering and headings/sub-headings must match what appears on the agenda document. It's vitally important that these documents are accurately aligned to each other for audit purposes.

Even if you create summary minutes with a full or objectives agenda, the minutes will be a lengthy document.

**Handy hint:** the longer your putt off writing the minutes the more time-consuming the task will be as it becomes difficult to remember what was discussed.

# Exercise: To Minute or Not

This exercise is designed to help you decide what should and shouldn't be minuted.

### Instructions:

Read the two scenarios below and then answer the questions relating to each scenario.

### Scenario 1:
During a board (formal) meeting a contentious motion is passed by the members. After a lengthy debate the majority agreed to dismiss a senior member of staff. This senior member of staff is not present at the board meeting.

One of the board members is very unhappy with the decision. He demands that his negative vote is recorded in the minutes. He also wants his reasons for voting against the motion to be recorded word-for-word. Finally, he wants to be named in the minutes.

Answer the following questions:

1. Should the member's comments be recorded word-for-word?

2. Should the member's name be included in the minutes?

3. What should be minuted if you decide not to record the comments word-for-word?

**Scenario 2:**
You are chairing a multi-departmental (business) meeting involving several senior managers.

One of the groups brings a written statement to the meeting. In it she is very critical of another group member. Her statement raises doubt about her colleague's honesty, integrity, motives and competence in the role. The statement is not only critical, it also contains unsubstantiated allegations. The member is asking for her statement to be included in the minutes.

Answer the following questions:

1. Should the written statement be attached to the minutes?

2. If you decide not to include the statement what should be minuted?

3. Who decides what should go into the minutes?

You will find the answers to this exercise in the Appendices section at the end of the book.

# 11.5 Approving and Issuing the Minutes

Although the minute taker has done all the work, the chairperson is the owner of the minutes. The chairperson should approve the minutes before they are issued.

The minute taker should create a full set of draft minutes before issuing them to the chairperson for review and approval. To ensure the minutes are ready for approval, use the following checklist:

1. Each agenda item includes a summary of the discussion (unless you are creating action point minutes)

2. The minutes are written in the third person, and there is no reference to individual attendees

3. The minutes are written in clear and concise English

4. Details of all the actions are included

5. The action owners have been recorded

6. There is a completion date for every action

If the chairperson fails to approve the minutes within five working days of the meeting, go ahead and issue the minutes. If there are any inaccuracies these will have to be dealt with at the next meeting.

## 11.6 Who Should Have a Copy of the Minutes?

Anyone who was invited to the meeting is automatically entitled to a copy of the minutes. This includes those people who sent apologies or failed to attend.

Anyone who wasn't invited to the meeting must seek the chairperson's permission. This is regardless of their seniority in the organisation. If anyone asks you to send them a copy of the minutes ask them to contact the chairperson.

If the minutes contain sensitive or confidential information the chairperson may decide to exercise his/her discretion and only issue the minutes to regular attendees. If the minutes contain sensitive or confidential information include a note to this effect in the covering email.

Once the minutes have been issued do not make any changes until the next meeting. It's common for attendees to send comments or ask the minutes to be amended, but the answer is always 'NO'.

**Handy hint:** Although minutes are a factual account of the meeting they shouldn't be unduly long. Don't feel compelled to write too many notes, or use all the notes you take during the meeting.

Once the minutes have been issued the minute taker's role is finished until the next meeting. The task of following up on the actions becomes the responsibility of the meeting secretary for the next meeting.

## Exercise: Creating Minutes Review

You now know the good practice regarding minutes. Use this opportunity to do a short review of your current working practices and decide what you are going to do differently in future.

**Instructions:**

Answer the following questions.

1. Do you currently follow the good practice guidelines i.e. matching headers and numbering for the agenda and minutes?

2. How quickly do you normally produce the minutes?

3. Have you identified any improvements you can make to your own minutes? If so, what are these?

4. Which style of minutes will you use in future?

5. What have you learnt about creating minutes that you didn't already know?

6. Are you going to find minute taking easier in future?

# Exercise: Meeting Case Study

**Overview:**
You have recently started working at 'The Only Way Is Up Ltd'; a business consultancy that employs 40 staff. You are employed as the PA to the Chief Executive. He formed the company five years ago.

The Chief Executive confirmed that he's an experienced meetings chairman and attendee. He recognises that good practice protocols exist but accepts that he doesn't always implement them. Some of his team don't know that protocol exists for meetings and minute taking.

Each month the Chief Executive has a meeting with his two fellow Directors, the Sales and Marketing Manager and 10 Sales and Marketing Consultants. The Chief Executive is always the chairman of this meeting. The aim of this meeting is to review how the business is getting on. The objectives for each meeting are:

1. Focus on existing customers (identify if we've lost any customers since the last meeting)

2. Is there anything we could have done to keep them?

3. Discuss new customers gained since the last meeting

4. Identify potential new customers and how we might secure their business

5. Consider ways to raise our profile and market ourselves better

As part of the meeting the group discusses customer queries, sales techniques that are or aren't working, and any areas of weakness in terms of performance. This is used to move the business forward.

This is your first meeting. You're an observer at this meeting so you can see how they operate. The Chief Executive has asked for your feedback at the end of the meeting. As a fresh pair of eyes, he thinks you may be able to see things they don't see.

The departing PA is the minute taker for this meeting. She is an excellent shorthand secretary and prides herself on her ability to capture everything that is said.

**Attendees:**
Chief Executive - Dennis Jackson (DJ)
Outgoing PA - Pamela Partridge (PP)
Director - Sara Higgins (SH)
Finance Director - Freddie Fiscal (FF)
Sales and Marketing Manager - Alexandros Stavros (AS)
Sales and Marketing Consultant - Rajesh Kumani (RK)
Sales and Marketing Consultant - Poppy Frankenstone (PF)
Sales and Marketing Consultant - Betty-Jean McBricker (BJM)
Sales and Marketing Consultant - Melville Muchrocks (MM)
Sales and Marketing Consultant - Lan Patel (LP)
Sales and Marketing Consultant - Hazel Sheppard (HS)
Sales and Marketing Consultant - Hugo Williams (HW)
Sales and Marketing Consultant - Sachiko Jaggers (SJ)
Sales and Marketing Consultant - Ricky Cobblehoff (RC)
Sales and Marketing Consultant - Lucy Chan (LC)

**Actions:**
The actions agreed during this meeting are:

1. We've lost one of our oldest clients in the last month. They said they could no longer afford our services. AS has an action to speak to the customer and see if we can get them back again

2. Everyone is to bring last month's and this month's sales reports to the next meeting

3. Each of the Sales Consultants has been asked to come up with a plan for getting three new clients before the end of the year. Alexandros Stavros is to work with the team and create an action plan for discussion at the next meeting

## Your Observations:

Your observations are:

1. The previous meeting in the boardroom had over-run and they hadn't tidied up at the end of the meeting. This gave the minute taker very little time to prepare for this meeting

2. The chairman arrived 10 minutes late. No-one commented or seemed to mind

3. As the chairman was late he skipped the 'Welcome and administration' agenda item. He was keen to make up some of the lost time

4. The agenda was handed out at the start of the meeting

5. Melville Muchrocks and Lan Patel didn't turn up, but didn't send their apologies either. No one knew why they were absent. Everyone else was present

6. Most of the attendees had forgotten to bring copies of last month's sales reports. The chairman decided to adjourn this item until the next meeting

7. Part way through the meeting Pamela, the outgoing PA, was asked to serve coffee. No-one took any notes while this was happening so there was a gap in the notes for the minutes

8. You notice that the first action doesn't have a completion date

## Post-meeting:

After the meeting the chairman asked you what you thought of your first meeting with 'The Only Way Is Up Ltd'. He recognises that the company's meetings are sometimes chaotic. He said this was as a result of the company growing faster than expected.

They didn't have the funds to provide formal meetings and minute taking training for staff when the company started. Now there isn't time to send staff on a formal training course as everyone is needed to cope with the workload.

The Chief Executive thinks it's time for the company to become more professional in the way it handles meetings. He recognises that the company if probably wasting time and money in some instances. He wants to start with this meeting and then roll out new working practices for all company meetings.

## Your Task:

The Chief Executive knows you are an experienced meeting secretary and minute taker. He would value your feedback on the following. The Chief Executive would like you to present your findings in a short report. How you choose to present your report is up to you.

1. Explain what was wrong with the meeting you attended

2. The chairman would like you to confirm the meeting secretary's role. He wants to share this information with all the staff to help them plan better meetings

3. Create a basic agenda template that can be used for all future company meetings

4. Create a minutes template that can be used for all future company meetings

5. Suggest the style of minutes the company should use for future meetings

6. Create a set of minutes for the actions from this meeting

This case study is an opportunity to reflect on what you already knew and to confirm what you've learnt from this book.

# 12. Freedom of Information Act

The Freedom of Information Act 2000 gives UK citizens the right to ask any public body for all the information they have on any subject they choose. The Freedom of Information (Scotland) Act 2002 covers the public bodies that the Holyrood parliament has jurisdiction over.

The Freedom of Information and Privacy Act is the United States equivalent. For other countries type https://en.wikipedia.org/wiki/Freedom_of_information_laws_by_country. Select the country from the list available.

The media frequently uses this right to obtain information that forms the basis of news stories. Unless there is a good reason not to, the organisation must provide the information within 20 working days.

Anyone can make a request for information, and you can ask for any information you like. There are no restrictions on age, nationality or where you live. Some information may be withheld to protect various interests that are allowed by the Act. If information is withheld the public authority must tell you why they have not shared this information.

You can also ask for any personal information the organisation holds about you. If you ask for information about yourself, then your request will be dealt with under the Data Protection Act 1998.

From a minute taker's point of view the Freedom of Information Act and the Data Protection Act can present a major challenge. When creating minutes carefully consider how much information should be recorded (particularly if you work in the public sector).

## 12.1 The Public Sector

If you work in the public sector be aware of the impact the Freedom of Information Act may have on your role. We are only dealing with the Act in respect of meetings and minute taking. You will need to do your own research to find out how the Act impacts your role more broadly.

The Freedom of Information Act applies to all public bodies. These include:

1. Government departments. The list is extensive. Type 'How to make a freedom of information request' into your search engine for details of the departments

2. Local authorities and councils

3. Schools colleges and universities

4. Health trusts, hospitals and doctors' surgeries

5. Publicly owned companies

6. Publicly funded museums

7. The police

## 12.2 What is Covered by the Freedom of Information Act?

The Freedom of Information Act requires every public authority to have a 'publication scheme'. This has to be approved by the Information Commissioner's Officer (ICO), and has to include the information covered by the scheme.

In short, this scheme means that certain classes of information must be routinely available to the public. This includes policies and procedures, minutes of meetings, annual reports and financial information.

If you would like to know more about what is covered by the Freedom of Information Act, please refer to the Information Commissioner's website (http://ico.org.uk).

## 12.3 Exempt Information

As I've already stated anyone can request information held by a public authority. This doesn't mean you will always receive all the information you ask for though. If there is a good reason to refuse the request, some information can be withheld.

There are three reasons why public authorities may refuse an entire request. These reasons are:

1. It would cost too much or take too many staff to deal with the request

2. The request is deemed to be vexatious

3. The request repeats a previous request from the same person

There are also various reasons for a public authority only providing limited information. If you would like to know more please refer to the Information Commissioner's website (http://ico.org.uk).

Even though you may not have to disclose a full copy of your minutes do take care when minuting discussions.

## 12.4 Useful Websites

If you work in a role where your meetings and minutes may be subject to the Freedom of Information Act you may find the following websites helpful.

The Freedom of Information Act:

United Kingdom - http://www.gov.uk

Scotland - http://www.scotland.gov.uk

United States - http://www.foia.gov/

The Information Commission:

United Kingdom - http://www.ico.gov.uk/

Scotland - http://www.itspublicknowledge.info

United States Information Agency - http://www.dosfan.lib.uic.edu/usia/

**Handy hint:** If your minutes contain confidential information make a reference indicating where this can be found. If you receive a freedom of information request you will be able to identify and remove the confidential information easily.

# 13. Conclusion

Meeting time is expensive, but well planned and executed meetings add value to businesses. This represents the pay-off (one of the five P's). There is no need for any meeting to be a waste of company time and money.

Proper planning and preparation will ensure your meeting has a real purpose. Meetings should never take place just because 'it seems like a good idea'. The thought that goes into the planning stage also ensures the right people attend the meeting.

Obviously the chairperson and minute taker play the key roles in meetings. However, each attendee should also have something to contribute. Never attend a meeting just because you've been invited, or may be able to contribute in some way. Know what is expected of you and the value you can add to the meeting.

Have you ever been guilty of issuing the agenda late or, worse still, not at all? Hopefully you now recognise the benefits of issuing the agenda in a timely manner.

One of the most common mistakes is numbering mismatch between the agenda and minutes. Strangely, often the document creator doesn't think about ensuring the numbering on the two documents matches. Perhaps it's the internal auditor in me that makes this seem obvious.

The agenda and minutes should be filed together as this makes the task of internal auditing much easier.

Perhaps you were considering abandoning face-to-face meetings in favour of virtual meetings. Hopefully the pros and cons in chapter 10 will give you food for thought. Clearly there are benefits with face-to-face and virtual meetings.

If you're a single office organisation then there is probably no need for virtual meetings. If you are a multi-office organisation you may find a combination of face-to-face and virtual meetings is the best option. The general rule is one size doesn't fit all.

Of course we shouldn't forget the world of apps. Nowadays there really is an app for everything in business. Some traditionalists feel there is no room for apps in meetings. Others believe apps are the way forward and we should all embrace them wholeheartedly.

I hope this book has provided you with some little nuggets of information to make your meeting time efficient and cost-effective. If you have any comments, observations or questions about meetings I would be delighted to hear from you.

Shepherd Creative Learning welcomes feedback, positive or negative. If you would like to get in touch with us our email address is shepherdcreativelearning@gmail.com.

I will allow Peter Drucker and John Kenneth Galbraith to have the final word. Hopefully you won't follow John Kenneth Galbraith's example.

"Time is the scarcest resource and unless it's managed nothing else can be managed". Peter Drucker (writer, professor, management consultant and self-described social ecologist).

"Meetings are indispensable when you don't want to do anything". John Kenneth Galbraith (Canadian economist, public official, and diplomat).

## Exercise: Meetings and Minute Taking Quiz

By now you probably feel you know all about meetings and minute taking. Why not test your knowledge with this quick quiz?

1. How many styles of agenda are there? Name each style of agenda

2. Which style of agenda is commonly used for business meetings?

3. How quickly should the minutes be issued following a monthly meeting?

4. If you discover errors in the minutes from the previous meeting, when should they be amended - before the next meeting/at the next meeting/not at all?

5. Name the four roles involved in meetings. One of these may not apply to every meeting

6. For monthly or less regular meetings when should the agenda be issued?

7. Do you need to have an agenda for every meeting?

8. Which documents should be issued with the agenda?

9. How should the person creating the agenda deal with late agenda items?

10. Should minutes contain details of who made specific comments?

11. What are the reasons for creating a separate agenda for the chairperson?

12. What is the difference between 'Apologies' and 'Absent'?

13. What is the purpose of the chairperson/minute taker briefing session?

14. Who is entitled to receive a copy of the minutes?

15. What is the set order for agenda items?

16. Do you have to include every agenda item I get a request for? If not, what criteria should you apply?

17. Is it acceptable to keep carrying actions forward from one meeting to the next?

18. Do you need to stick to the order of the agenda during the meeting, or can you switch things around?

19. How should you record who was present and who was absent?

20. If you are invited to a meeting do you need to attend?

You will find the answers to these questions in the Appendices section at the end of the book.

# 14. Terms

The terms in this chapter can relate to formal, business and informal meetings.

Absent - These are the people who were expected to attend the meeting. They didn't turn up or send their apologies

Any other business - This is an agenda item for emergency use only. This is an opportunity to discuss urgent matters that came to light after the agenda was issued

Attendees - This can be anyone attending the meeting. This includes the chairperson, minute taker, attendees, visitors or observers

Chairperson - The person running the meeting. This is not necessarily the most senior person in the room

Chairperson's brief - This is also known as the chairperson's agenda. It's simply a more detailed agenda than the version issued to the other attendees

Contributors - These are also referred to as attendees. These can be people who attended all or part of the meeting. As the name suggests they are expected to contribute to the meeting in some way. Anyone who doesn't contribute and isn't there as an observer should leave/not attend in future

Declarations of interest - These are a potential conflict of interest relating to one (or more) of the agenda items. Declarations of interest should be declared at the start of the meeting

In attendance - This term is used for formal meetings only. The term refers to people present, who aren't board members

Matters arising - These are the actions from the previous meeting. Ideally each action should be closed at the current meeting, not carried forward to future meetings

Meeting secretary - The person creating and issuing the agenda and other documents for discussion at the meeting. Note: often the meeting secretary and minute taker are the same person

Minutes of the previous meeting - These are the minutes from the previous meeting. At the current meeting, these minutes will be adopted or amended

Minute taker - The person responsible for taking notes in the meeting and creating and issuing the minutes

Observers - People who have been invited to observe the meeting. Only the chairperson should invite observers. Observers are not permitted to participate in the meeting, but they should be there for a specific reason e.g. future minute taker

Substitutes - These are people who are deputising for a regular member of the group, who is unable to attend. Substitutes are expected to participate in the discussions are far as possible. Otherwise there is no point in them attending the meeting

Visitors - These are people who don't normally attend the meeting. They have usually been invited to deliver a presentation, lead a discussion or contribute to a specific agenda item. Visitors aren't normally expected to stay for the entire meeting

# 15. Appendices

In this chapter you will find the answers to the exercises earlier in the book.

## 15.1 Exercise: Meetings - Quick Quiz - Answers

Here are the answers to the quick quiz you completed in chapter 1. See how you fared.

1. Answer - False. It's generally the person who decided to call the meeting, unless they decide to delegate the task to someone else

2. Answer - True. The key skills of a good chairperson are - good time management skills, an excellent communicator, assertiveness skills, ability to ensure decisions are made during the meeting, accurately record actions, flexible approach and impartial

3. Answer - False. Good shorthand secretaries don't automatically make good minute takers as the two roles require different skills. Some shorthand secretaries can comfortably fulfil both roles

4. Answer - False. There is a standard order for agenda. This is - Apologies, Welcome, introductions and administration, Minutes of the previous meeting, Matters arising, Reports,

Main agenda items, Any other business and Date of next meeting

5. Answer - False. The minute taker should be the person most capable of stepping up to the role. For the purpose of the meeting the minute taker is part of the management team. If everyone understands this they will probably have a far greater respect for the minute taker and minute taking as a role

6. Answer - False. The minutes should be issued within five working days of the meeting (for monthly or less frequent meetings). The agenda should be issued at least four working days before the next meeting

7. Answer - False. Although 'Apologies' is listed as the first item on the agenda, this item is not numbered

8. Answer - False. Only people who sent their apologies or those who were on holiday or sick leave should be recorded as having sent their apologies. Anyone who just doesn't turn up is recorded as 'Absent' or 'Did not attend'

9. Answer - False. Minutes provide an accurate audit trail of the meeting. In some circumstances the minutes may be subject to a Freedom of Information Act request

10. Answer - Three of each. These are basic, full and objectives agenda. Summary, verbatim and action point minutes

So how did you get on? Were you pleased or disappointed with your score?

# 15.2 Exercise: To Minute or Not - Answers

Here are the answers to the To Minute or Not exercise in chapter 11. Your choice of wording may be slightly different, but here is the information that should have been captured for the minutes:

### Scenario 1:

1. No. The minutes should be a summary of what was discussed, not a record of what was said. You would only make a word-for-word record if it was a disciplinary meeting with the senior member of staff

2. The rules of minute taking are clear - people should never be named in the minutes

3. The minutes should be a summary of the discussion. The minutes should confirm that a motion has been passed to dismiss [name of the senior staff member]. For future reference it might be helpful to confirm why the motion to dismiss has been passed

### Scenario 2:

1. No. There are unsubstantiated claims in this document. Minuting this could lead to a grievance from the injured party

2. Do not name the person making the statement. Depending on what is discussed you may need to name the person the statement is about. Check with the chairperson

3. The chairperson is responsible for deciding what should be minuted. Due to the contentious nature of this discussion minute as little information as possible

# 15.3 Exercise: Meetings and Minute Taking Quiz - Answers

Here are the answers to the quick quiz you completed in chapter 13. See how you fared.


1. There are three styles of agenda. These are basic agenda, full agenda and objectives agenda

2. The basic agenda is commonly used for business meetings

3. The minutes should be issued within five working days of the meeting. It's important that the minute taker and chairperson give priority to this task

4. The errors should be dealt with at the next meeting. The amendments can be made to the minutes and the revised document stored with the old one. The original minutes should not be reissued but a note should be included in the minutes for this meeting

5. The four roles are chairperson, minute taker, attendee and observer. Not all meetings have observers

6. The agenda should be issued at least five working days before the meeting. This gives everyone time to prepare for the meeting

7. Yes, you should have an agenda for formal and business meetings. You may decide not to have an agenda for informal meetings, but you should have a list of topics for discussion

8. Any reports or other documents to be discussed during the meeting should be issued with the agenda. It's unreasonable and unrealistic to issue reports during the meeting and expect to have a meaningful discussion

9. If you receive late agenda item requests you need to establish whether it absolutely must be discussed at the meeting. The normal course of action is to reject the request for this meeting but offer to include it in the agenda for the next meeting

10. Never name people who made comments during the meeting. Aside being bad practice, you will discourage people from contributing to the meeting as no one wants to see their comments in writing

11. The chairperson's agenda is much more detailed than the version issued to everyone else. This helps the chairperson during the meeting. It should include timings, highlights what is required from each agenda item and any other useful background information

12. Only people who sent their apologies or those who were on holiday or sick leave should be recorded as having sent their apologies. Anyone who just doesn't turn up is recorded as 'Absent' or 'Did not attend'

13. The purpose of this meeting is to discuss the content of the meeting and any updates. It's also about any help either party might need during the meeting

14. Everyone who was invited to the meeting, whether they attended or not, is entitled to a copy of the minutes. If anyone else wants a copy they should ask the chairperson's permission

15. The order for agenda items is - Apologies, Welcome, Minutes of the previous meeting, Matters arising, Reports, Main agenda items, Any other business, and Date of next meeting

16. Don't feel you must include agenda items just because you have been asked to. Agenda items need to be relevant to the overall purpose of the meeting. It also needs to be relevant to the majority of attendees

17. Ideally every action should be closed at the following meeting. This isn't always possible for various reasons. Allow actions to be carried forward once if necessary. After that close the action down and write a covering not in the minutes to explain what has happened. If you keep carrying actions forward you will create messy minutes and an unclear audit trail

18. Always stick to the order of the agenda items, unless there is an exceptionally good reason not to. The order of the agenda items should have been considered when creating the agenda

19. Start with those present, and then record apologies followed by absent. Always name the chairperson first, followed by the minute taker. After this I name people in alphabetical order by last name as this is the most efficient way to record the information

20. Only attend a meeting if you have something to contribute. If you don't know why you've been invited, ask the chairperson

www.ingramcontent.com/pod-product-compliance
Lightning Source LLC
Chambersburg PA
CBHW050547280326
41933CB00011B/1750